SELLING THE ARSENAL OF DEMOCRACY

AMERICA'S WEAPONS OF WORLD WAR II AS SEEN IN HOMEFRONT MAGAZINES

GLENN A. KNOBLOCK

FONTHILL

In memory of my grandfather, Frederick J. Knoblock, 216th Combat Engineers Battalion, 16th Armored Division, and the 1st Infantry Division, World War II.

And
My Great Aunt, Gertrude Knoblock Danby, Yeoman 1c (F) U.S. Navy, Lake Torpedo Boat Company, World War I, U.S. Coast Guard, Miami, Florida, World War II.

SEA WOLF *with Fangs of Fire!*

OFFICIAL INSIGNE
OF ONE OF THE
CARRIER-BASED SQUADRONS
UNITED STATES NAVY

This insigne was specially created by the Walt Disney Studios for the men of the "Sea Wolf" Squadron. They carry it on their planes, the famous cannon-firing Curtiss Helldivers.

COPYRIGHT WALT DISNEY

Take a group of alert, aggressive, fighting-mad, young Americans. Give them all the flying and fighting "know how" the Navy can provide. Equip them with the very latest of dive-bombers . . . the Curtiss Helldiver . . . a "triple-threat warplane" that can bomb, or strafe, or fight. Then turn these men and their planes and their Fire-Power loose in Axis skies . . . roaring down to plant their bombs on enemy carriers . . . sweeping back to clear the decks with high-explosive cannon shell . . . There you have a perfect picture of the "Sea Wolves" . . . a fast-flying, straight-shooting, hard-hitting squadron that's typical of America's fighting Navy!

We at Oldsmobile have long been associated with the production of Fire-Power for the Army—cannon for planes, tanks and tank destroyers, shell for the artillery and armored forces. Only now, however, can it be told to what extent Oldsmobile is producing for the Navy, too. The famous Curtiss Helldiver, for example, carries Oldsmobile-built automatic aircraft cannon in its wings. Other well-known Navy planes, such as the Corsair fighter and Vega Ventura bomber, are powered with Pratt and Whitney engines, the same type for which Oldsmobile produces vital parts. And the Navy's surface forces have long been using high-explosive shell from Oldsmobile. Fire-Power is Our Business, and horsepower, too . . . *for both Army and Navy!*

HELP OUR CARRIERS CARRY ON!

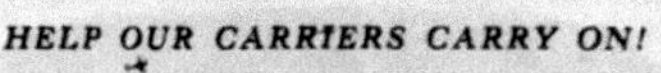

The great task forces of the U. S. Navy are fighting their most critical battles in the enemy's very backyard. That takes courage, and skill . . . and *money!*

Buy War Bonds!

OLDSMOBILE DIVISION OF **GENERAL MOTORS**

FIRE-POWER IS OUR BUSINESS

Fonthill Media Language Policy

Fonthill Media publishes in the international English language market. One language edition is published worldwide. As there are minor differences in spelling and presentation, especially with regard to American English and British English, a policy is necessary to define which form of English to use. The Fonthill Policy is to use the form of English native to the author. Glenn A. Knoblock was born in Parma Heights, Ohio, and educated at Bowling Green State University, Bowling Green, Ohio; therefore American English has been adopted in this publication.

Fonthill Media Limited
Fonthill Media LLC
www.fonthill.media
books@fonthill.media

First published in the United Kingdom and the United States of America 2022

British Library Cataloguing in Publication Data:
A catalogue record for this book is available from the British Library

ISBN 978-1-78155-863-8

Typeset in 10pt on 13pt Sabon LT
Printed and bound in England

Contents

Introduction

Have you ever come across an old magazine from the 1940s, whether at a local thrift or antique shop, in your grandparent's house, or, more likely, in some online forum or marketplace? If so, several things will have caught your attention, perhaps the "old-fashioned" articles, or maybe their large 11 by 14 format, a size that was perfect for publications like *Life* magazine to feature their many award-winning photographs and illustrations. However, for most of us, the first thing that catches our eye are the advertisements. These feature period clothes and hairstyles that have long been out of fashion, car brands that have long ago disappeared from American dealerships, or even personal care products and other brands that we still know today but in a much different form. However, for those magazines that were published in America between 1942 and 1945, the one real eye-catcher are those advertisements related to World War II. Perhaps the most surprising ads in this category are those that featured actual weapons of war, and that is what this book is all about. *Selling the Arsenal of Democracy* tells the full story of these ads, the weapons America used to defeat the Axis powers in World War II, both what they depicted in realistic fashion and the real story behind the weapons themselves, but also what they meant on the home front economically, as well as what they represented symbolically. Never before, and never since World War II, had America advertised her weapons of war for all to see in such a broad, bold, and expansive fashion. There is a lot to "read" in these advertisements, and, indeed, what they say tells us a lot about the American mindset during the war. This book, however, not only discusses the facts behind these advertisements, but also presents a history of each of these weapons themselves. These histories help to put their wartime contribution into perspective from a non-technical standpoint and are meant for the general reader.

For many, the color illustrations in this book will be interesting, powerful, and certainly mind-opening. For those readers who are old enough to have lived during the war, or even veterans who fought in it, the images will likely be both nostalgic and bittersweet. For the Baby Boomers, the children of those who lived through World War II, it will be a reminder of what their parents experienced or perhaps even the stories they heard tell of. However, for those to whom World War II is just an event they learned about in history class, or a war in which a relative fought who died long before they were ever born, this book will, hopefully, be even more insightful. As the grandson of a man, one of the biggest influences in my life, who was a World War II armored veteran, and the great-nephew of an equally influential woman who served in both World War I and World War II in the Navy and Coast Guard, it perhaps was inevitable that I would write this book. I first became aware that ads like these existed, sometime in the late 1970s, when I stumbled across a couple of old magazines in a local bookstore and was fascinated by what I saw. I knew World War II history well by this time, but not like this. Later on, after I gained my history degree, I began to slowly collect these advertisements, and have been doing so, off and on now, for the past thirty years. Sometimes they have been framed and on display in my office, but mostly they have sat unused, awaiting the time when they could be displayed or used in a better way. Long ago, I decided to write a book about them, and now, twenty books later, it finally seemed like I better get to it. With the men and women of that Greatest Generation fast leaving us, it is about time, once again, that we see the war, at least in a small way, as they and their relatives did on the home front.

Part I

SELLING THE WAR ON THE HOME FRONT

1

Advertising Basics during World War II

When America entered World War II after the disastrous attack on Pearl Harbor, our country was woefully unprepared. As late as 1939, we had only the thirty-ninth largest army in the world (Brazil's was larger), and our cavalry force was still ordering saddles, while the numbers of tanks in our arsenal paled in comparison to that of countries like Germany, France, and even Great Britain. As for the Army Air Force (this was before the Air Force became a separate branch of our armed forces), many of our planes were at best inadequate, and at worst functionally obsolete. True, more aircraft were on the way after President Roosevelt and the Congress came to terms, but they were slow in coming, and though about 2,500 airplanes of all kinds were being built monthly in January 1941, it would not be enough to both help supply our allies in Europe, as well as our own forces to fight a vast, two-front war. As to shipbuilding, here too the United States lagged behind. The United States Maritime Commission began the Emergency Shipbuilding Program in late 1940, but in all of 1941, only seventy merchant ships were built to carry American goods worldwide to our allies and strategic bases. Indeed, in his Fireside Chat on December 29, 1940, President Roosevelt told how the United States must become "the great arsenal of democracy," even though he had previously campaigned on a pledge to keep us out of the war that had broken out in Europe in 1939 when the Nazis invaded Poland. Now, after Pearl Harbor, less than two years later, staying out of the war was not an option; instead, it was all about how we would "win" the war. For Roosevelt, nothing had changed, and the "arsenal of democracy" was now, more than ever, the key to our survival, he telling Congress that "Powerful enemies must be out-fought and out-produced.... We must out-produce them overwhelmingly, so that there can be no question of our ability to provide a crushing superiority of equipment." And this is the course that Roosevelt set forth for America almost immediately; some commodities were quickly rationed within less than a week of the Pearl Harbor attack, primarily rubber, mainly in the form of car tires, due to the fact that the Japanese had captured rubber plantations on Indonesia formerly controlled by the Dutch. Shortly thereafter, on January 1, 1942, new car production in the United States was banned beginning in February. Almost every other commodity you can imagine (except eggs and dairy products) would be rationed in the near future, the first being sugar, but soon enough dog food and typewriters in March 1942, followed by bicycles in May, with prices frozen in that same month on many everyday items. In addition to the rationing program, war-time production and the conversion of factory production from regular civilian goods to items for the war effort was quickly undertaken, the War Production Board established in early 1942, and the Office of War Mobility in 1943. The effects of this incredible and massive effort to increase war-time production has been told many times over, but for our purpose here is well-worth reiterating—not only were everyday commodities rationed and often in short supply (both food and fuel), so too were such big-ticket items as cars, washing machines, sewing machines. Interestingly, some 30 percent of all cigarettes produced and 15 percent of beer production was allocated for the military, while whiskey was also in short supply as distilleries were harnessed and converted for the production of industrial alcohol that was used in torpedo fuel. Even those who had an automobile restricted travel in order to save fuel and tire wear, asked to drive at the "Victory Speed" limit of 35 mph, which explains how that figure has become a ubiquitous one in our driving history. In effect, the life of every single American during World War II was affected in some way, shape, or form. Now, closer to our topic, one might ask about the print media and their restrictions during wartime. As to paper supplies, this was never a major problem, as the U.S. manufactured about half of all the paper produced in the world in 1939. As with other commodities, paper production was controlled by the government, and wartime recycling initiatives, especially in the immediate aftermath of Pearl Harbor, were implemented, but early on there was actually a surplus of paper. While the wartime recycling drives contributed to the notion that there was a shortage of paper, this was far from the case. In fact, due to the opening of a number of paper mills, much of the recycled paper that was collected was stockpiled for later use. It is for this reason that American magazine, newspaper, and book production during the war, essential aspects of our freedom of speech ideals, was never seriously threatened or even curtailed, and a major reason why so many wartime era magazines have survived down to the present day. In fact, these magazines, along with newspapers, radio programs, and movie-reel news shows, were an essential component of keeping Americans informed of the war's progress, and what measures they at home could take to insure victory. However, it was not just the written articles that kept the citizens on the home front engaged, it was also the advertisements within, the joint products of ad-copy writers and illustrators working for major advertising agencies that helped, both on a conscience and unconscious level, to sell the war effort and America's role as the arsenal of democracy. What follows is a discussion of the various aspects of those advertisements that depicted weapons of war.

Censorship

The first question on many people's minds about these advertisements might be in regards to wartime censorships. After all, why did wartime restrictions not cover this type of information? It does not come as any surprise that on December 19, 1941, less than two weeks after the attack on Pearl Harbor, the Office of Censorship was established to control the dissemination of sensitive wartime information through the issuance of Executive Order 8985 by President Roosevelt. The practices of the Roosevelt administration and Byron Price, his director of censorship, were relatively tame and primarily consisted of the policy of voluntary censorship. This meant that news and other media organizations, magazines included, were to censor their own activities, with the responsibility falling on the media companies themselves for any failures. While the American Civil Liberties Union (ACLU) decried any censorship whatsoever, the Office of Censorship published guidelines for print media that were just a few pages long. Restricted information included troop movements, losses incurred by U.S. forces, wartime production figures, and sensitive weather information. For Director Price, his ongoing motto was "Least said, soonest mended." While the censorship activities were extensive in regards to cable and telephone communications, as well as postal mail and radio programs, the American print media largely complied willingly, the one major exception being the May Incident, which occurred in 1943. A statement by Kentucky Congressman Andrew Jackson May who, in June 1943, after visiting the Pacific war zone, revealed the information that the Submarine Force had been successful against the Japanese because of the fact that in submarine countermeasures, the Japanese were setting their depth-charges at too shallow of a setting, allowing for American submarines to escape destruction. As if this press conference was not bad enough, its contents were published by a number of newspaper outlets around the country, including the *Honolulu Star-Bulletin*, located in the town that was the home base of the American Pacific Fleet. This whole affair was later said to have resulted in the loss of approximately ten U.S. submarines and 800 submariners in all according to Vice Admiral Charles Lockwood, the commander of the Pacific Submarine Fleet. While it is impossible to know how many submarines were lost directly because of May's revelations for certain, his careless comments demonstrated an extreme example of poor judgement by someone who, as chairman of the committee on military affairs, should have known better, especially in light of the "Loose lips sink ships" ad campaign that was then in full force. Despite this incident, it is notable that May was never punished for his faulty judgement, which was no doubt unintentional in that he never meant to cause submariners harm.

In the end, the reason the weapons of war advertisements were allowable under censor regulations is the fact that though the depictions of such things as aircraft, tanks, and various armaments were realistic in pictorial form, no secrets as to their performance in regards to speed, altitude, and range were revealed. Though spies, as well as captured German submariners held in Canadian prison camps, tried to obtain any information they could through American magazine and news reports, it was just a reality that any information that might be learned by the Axis powers could soon enough be discerned on the battlefield. Just as American forces learned about the capabilities of the famed Japanese Zero fighter after an example was shot down in the Aleutian Islands in July 1942 (said to have been one of the greatest prizes during the war in the Pacific), subsequently being recovered and minutely examined, so too could the Germans and Japanese do this with U.S. aircraft shot down over land or U.S. tanks destroyed in battle. Instead, the depictions of these weapons of war served to buoy the confidence and outlook of American citizens on the home front. Not only did these powerful ads give tangible examples and information of the American force that would prevail overseas, but they also stirred in many a sense of patriotic pride, especially those men and women who helped build these weapons. In looking at these ads, family members of many a serviceman, perhaps a wife, could proudly point to a picture of, say, a P-38 Lightning fighter, and say "there, that's what my husband is flying to do his part to win the war."

Let The Enemy War Birds Come!

America's anti-aircraft guns are giving our planes real competition in the grim job of depleting enemy air power. Their range and accuracy mows down enemy aircraft, or keeps them at such altitudes that their bombs fall wide. Their flexibility and rapidity in action has proved disastrous for dive and torpedo bombers, and mounted for rapid mobility, they won their spurs in Tunisia and the South Pacific, where they proved devastating against ground as well as air forces.

Back of the deadly work of these modern-day guns is not only advanced design but staunch construction. The impacts and stresses of rapid fire are taken in stride by the toughest of forged parts. At Kropp Forge, we take pride in the vast quantities of rugged forgings we are turning out for anti-aircraft guns, planes, ships, tanks, military vehicles and essential war machinery.

The inquiries of armament builders for forgings of all types are solicited.

Kropp Forge Company
Makers of Drop, Upset and Hammer Forgings for Ships, Guns, Planes, Tanks, Ordnance and Machine Tools
"World's Largest Job Forging Shop"
5301 W. Roosevelt Road, Chicago, Ill.
Engineering Representatives in Principal Cities

Proudly we fly the Army and Navy "E" flag and stars, awarded and re-awarded for excellence and proficiency in the production of war materiel.

The War Advertising Council

In addition to government censorship policies that helped guide American media war-time standards, there was also a private industry group that guided its members as well. This was the Advertising Council, which was established in early 1941, ten months before Pearl Harbor, and was a group of advertising agencies who banded together to support the war effort. This group, which changed its name to the War Advertising Council in June 1943, ran public campaigns, which operated not only independently, but whose goals or themes were also embodied in individual advertisements created by their members for companies promoting their wartime goods or the weapons they built for the war effort. The organization's longest running campaign was for the war bond effort, beginning in 1942, encouraging Americans to buy these bonds to support the war effort, both in individual advertisements, as well as in stand-alone ads. Interesting examples of encouraging Americans to buy war bonds are found in the fine print in many weapons-themed ads—that for Champion Spark Plugs depicting an M-3 tank states "Keep 'em Rolling-Buy U.S. War Bonds and Stamps," while an ad for the Indian Motorcycle Company states "Buy War Bonds Now to Buy an Indian Later." Perhaps the best-known phrasing used to promote war bonds sales was that of "Back the Attack, Buy War Bonds," used on many weapons-themed ads. Another important ad campaign, the words still remembered today, was the "Loose Lips Sink Ships" campaign, which also began in 1942. This campaign also had a partner in the Stetson Company, famed for their cowboy hats, utilizing the saying "Keep it under your Stetson" as another way of advising citizens not to spread information that could harm the war effort and our soldiers and sailors overseas. The War Advertising Council continued under this name until 1946, when it returned to peace-time themes and changed its name back to the Advertising Council, informally known to this day as the Ad Council. Their efforts were so successful in raising awareness during the war that President Roosevelt, and Truman afterwards, asked the council to continue their work in peacetime. Interestingly, their longest-running initiative began in 1944 with Smokey the Bear as a spokesman for the prevention of forest fires campaign, while they are also responsible for well-known modern campaigns, including those against drunk driving, promoting seat-belt use, AIDS prevention, Autism Awareness, and many others.

Profit and Publicity

Another question that arises abouts these advertisements, and perhaps the most compelling, is what motivated the companies, both big and small, that either built these weapons of war, or the components used in their building, to place them? Why did they feel compelled to tout their work and, as is fair to ask of all paid advertising, what was in it for them to do so? In fact, there is more than one answer to this question, and they can be divided up into two closely-related categories, profit and publicity. Many advertisements during the war incorporate both of these elements in subtle ways. First, let us take a look at the profit element. Even during the war effort, companies were not fully and so strictly controlled by the U.S. government that they had no measure of freedom to decide what to produce. For example, President Roosevelt's chief of the Office of Production Management, later called the War Production Board beginning in January 1942, William Knudsen (a former auto-industry executive), knew that when it came to aircraft production, car companies like General Motors, Hudson, Studebaker, and others would have the best facilities for production conversion. The Ford Motor Company in particular was asked in 1941 to build sub-assemblies for the B-24 Liberator bomber, a large and complex airplane. However, Henry Ford declined, basically telling the OPM that Ford would either build the whole airplane, or nothing at all. Knudsen had no choice in the matter, but the decision by Ford to stand his ground by dictating the terms of what he would build was not only the correct one, but one with historic implications. Ford Motor would subsequently build their huge, 4.7-million-square-foot Willow Run aircraft factory, with the largest indoor factory floor in the world in Ypsilanti, Michigan, in 1941 and began producing B-24 Liberator bombers by the fall of 1942. After finally gaining full control from the B-24's original designer, Consolidated Aircraft Company of San Diego, as well as ironing-out their own production problems. Willow Run would go on to build nearly 7,000 B-24s, a bomber that was key to the war effort.

Civilian manufacturing companies turned weapon's manufacturers not only gained a direct tax break for producing their print advertisements (which also touted the sales of war bonds), but their civilian brand name also received a boost, the value of which is hard to calculate in terms of real dollars, in several different ways. The first was rather broad in nature and was directly related to the Wall Street Crash of 1929 and resulting Great Depression. During this time period, with many individuals out of work and families struggling to survive and purchasing power drastically lowered, corporate America had a huge public-relations problem, with corporate greed blamed for the current disaster. Likewise, has been often true throughout history, the advertising industry was held in low regard during the 1930s in regards to their considered dishonest practices. The part these corporate giants, once vilified, played in building the arsenal of democracy and winning the war was undeniable and making these efforts known to the general public through advertising was an important way to burnish a previously tarnished image.

In addition to any short-term value to be gained from these advertisements, the touting of their building these weapons of war was also a strategic move for the future, Whether it was Chrysler, Cadillac, the Singer Sewing Machine Company, or the well-known Kelvinator refrigerator company, most of these companies products were either not as readily available or could not be purchased at all during the war because production had been shifted to non-consumer goods for the war effort. So, why advertise for products that could not be purchased? In a play for future business in the post-war era, many company's ads included wording that spoke to that time when the war would be over, and then their products would be available. The Graham-Paige Auto Company of Detroit advertised that "And when Graham-Paige war equipment has done its share in earning Victory," their name "will appear on modern automobiles, farm tractors, and farm machinery for peacetime America." In similar fashion, the United States Steel Company depicts in one advertisement the bazookas made out of their steel alongside four household appliances, including a toaster and an iron, stating about their "quality steel" and products to come that "they'll be made into products for *you* when peace comes." Whatever the company involved, it was their hope that consumers in the immediate post-war economy would remember these advertisements and the contributions they made to the war effort that were highlighted, and subsequently turn these memories into purchasing dollars. Whether such a play was successful for most companies is uncertain and unmeasurable in most cases. Despite the fact that the above-mentioned Graham-Paige Auto Company lasted less than two years after the war as an auto manufacturer, the larger car companies like General Motors, Ford, Chrysler, and Studebaker very likely achieved some benefit from their war-time production among consumers, including many returning G.I.s who became buyers once again. It is likely that the tank man who drove an Oldsmobile or Chrysler-powered Sherman tank through the war may have been inclined to buy his new car from that very same company, likewise the man who served as a crewman or pilot in a Ford-built B-24 Liberator or a Studebaker-built B-17 Flying Fortress may have been compelled to purchase a car of this same make and model in peacetime. No doubt this is what manufacturers hoped for in the future. The largest success story in this regard, however, is that of the Willys-Overland Motor Company of Toledo, Ohio, which helped develop the famed jeep during the war, and afterwards turned it into a civilian vehicle brand all their own.

Finally, when it came to motivation, these advertisements were not just meant for consumers, or future consumers. They were also intended to be viewed by the many factory workers who built these weapons of war and served as both a source of pride in print for the valuable work that they were doing, as well as an inspiration to these men and women to work even harder to produce even more wartime goods. If you look closely, many wartime advertisements feature prominently an Army-Navy E flag, which was an honor presented to those companies by the Armed Forces for achieving "Excellence in Production." This award had first been used separately by the two branches of the Armed Forces beginning in 1906, the Army A Award and the Navy E Award, and remained separate awards until they were merged into one in July 1942. The criteria involved all aspects of manufacturing, including quality and quantity of items produced, as well as proper training, fair labor practices, a good health and safety record, and an avoidance of work stoppages due to strikes or obstacles in the production process. This was a very prestigious award, and only 5 percent of the approximately 85,000 companies that produced wartime goods were ever so honored. Once the honor was granted, a ceremony was held at the plant, attended by military personnel, factory or company management as well as their workers. The Army-Navy E pennant was presented to the company, while workers were given a pin or some other type of insignia to wear. Of course, local newspaper coverage of this award was extensive. When future production goals were met, the company and its workers were eligible for an additional star award every six months for maintaining the production criteria. To gain the star award in addition to the initial E Award was

SESSIONS

THE SUN NEVER SETS ON THE FIGHTING JEEP

U. S. MARINES CRASH SOLOMON ISLES

IN JEEPS FROM WILLYS-OVERLAND

ON the shores of Guadalcanal and on the beach at Tulagi Bay, the fearless, hard-boiled U. S. Marines speeded their attack with modern Willys Jeeps.

In the hands of men like these, the tough fighting Jeep now adds new drive and mobility to a striking power already famous throughout the world. The jabbering Japs in the Solomons found this out when husky U. S. Marines charged up the beaches with their rugged Willys Jeeps and cleared the enemy out of those strategic bases needed for our advance in the far Pacific.

The Willys Jeep is outstanding among the various types of superior equipment being produced for our fighting forces and those of our allies by American manufacturing genius.

Willys-Overland civilian engineers, working with the U. S. Quartermaster Corps, designed and perfected the Willys Jeep adopted as standard by the U. S. Army. The amazing, world-renowned GO-DEVIL engine that drives it with such power, speed and flexibility, is an exclusive development of Willys-Overland Motors, Inc.

Buy More U. S. War Stamps and Bonds

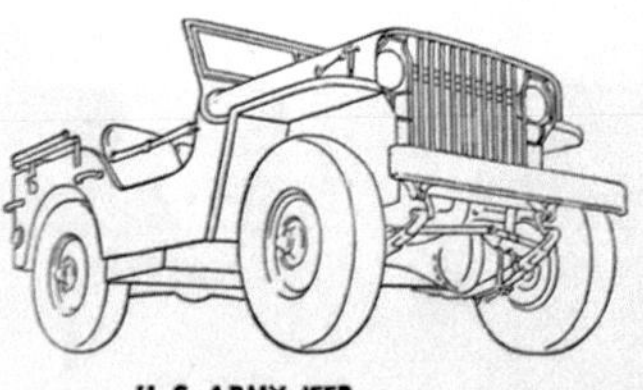

U. S. ARMY JEEP

WILLYS

MOTOR CARS TRUCKS AND JEEPS

AMERICAR—the People's Car

THE GO-DEVIL ENGINE—power-heart of WILLYS CARS and all JEEPS

TO THE SEVEN SEAS

of a War-Torn World

HIGGINS INDUSTRIES sends forth its products to the fighting forces of the United Nations—

On land, on sea, and in the air.

In the last year Higgins Industries has established the greatest boat production in the history of the world.

Today boats and other products move in an ever-increasing stream from nine Higgins plants, each of which was set up and put into operation without a cent of government aid.

Ask the Commandos on the shores of France and Norway

Ask the Marines in the Solomon Islands

In Iceland and in Africa

In the Aleutians and in the Coral Sea

"higgins boat" means Dependability.

HIGGINS INDUSTRIES, INC.

NEW ORLEANS, LA.

WORLD'S LARGEST BUILDERS OF BOATS

NOVEMBER, 1942

Landing Boat

The "Crocodile"↑ ↓Coast Guard Patrol Boat

Anti-Submarine Boat↑ ↓Tank Carrier

HIGGINS ALSO PRODUCES:

Steel and Wood Tugboats and Barges
Amphibious Equipment
Torpedo Tubes
Power Gun Turrets
Sound Communicating Devices
Paratroop Radio Telephone
Cut Crystals
Smoke Generators
Water Purifiers and Salt Water Converters
Engine Clutch and Reverse Gear Mechanism
Hypoid & Helican Gears
Bonded Wood,—Plastics
Lifeboat Releasing Gears
Turbine Type Pumps
Remote Engine Controls
Mechanical Steering Devices
Higite, (new explosive)
Twin Machine Gun, Cannon Stabilizer and Sighting Control

THE SECRETARY OF THE NAVY
WASHINGTON

DEAR MR. HIGGINS:

This is to inform you that the Army and Navy are conferring upon the Industrial Canal, City Park, and Bayou St. John Plants of Higgins Industries, the Army-Navy Production Award for high achievement in the production of war equipment.

This award symbolizes your country's appreciation of each man and woman in these plants. Accorded only to those organizations which have shown exceptional performance in fulfilling their tasks, it consists of a flag to be flown above your company, and a lapel pin which each individual may wear as a sign of distinguished service to his country.

I am confident that your outstanding record will bring victory nearer by inspiring others to similar high achievement.

Sincerely yours,
FRANK KNOX (Signed)

1

very difficult and something even fewer companies achieved. In the end, it is not hard to imagine a male factory worker, or perhaps a housewife turned Rosie the Riveter, after a tired day at work in an aircraft or tank factory, reading one of their employer's ads in a publication like *Collier's*, *Popular Mechanic*, or *The Saturday Evening Post*, and gaining some small sense of satisfaction.

Everyday Items Go Off to War

One of the most fascinating aspects of our wartime economy and the advertising that went along with it is the fact that even for those items that were available for home front use or consumption, they also could be advertised as helping to win the war in some way, shape, or form. This was most commonly highlighted in the form of supporting such initiatives as war bond drives, but also in more novel and humorous ways. The charming ad for Rice Krispies featuring a PT boat is an excellent example, the cereal handy enough to have "on hand for instant duty 'round the clock," and to help those who had "Days crowded with war work-nights too." In other cases, consumer products were transformed by ad copy into essential items, which would aid our soldiers and help win the war. In the case of such companies as the Gruen Watch Company, Bausch & Lomb Optical, or Kodak, their precision-built consumer goods, while still available at home, were also ones that had a military application. The Kodak Company offers an excellent example: their film products were readily available during the war, as were some of their civilian cameras. However, the company also manufactured the AN-N6 gun camera, which was the most widely used camera by the U.S. military during the war. Electronically operated, the camera, typically mounted in the wings of a fighter or bomber, was activated automatically when a pilot fired his weapons, recording the combat results of a mission. Another, more disastrous example, of a "weaponized" consumer product is demonstrated by the humorous and misleading ad for Nestle's chocolate brand of the Type D Emergency Ration bar carried by American soldiers early in the war. This ration, consisting of a 4-ounce block of chocolate, really was part of a soldier's rations until it was discontinued in 1943. First conceived by the Army in 1937 and manufactured by Hershey, this "chocolate" bar consisted of cacao fat mixed with oat flour and was able to withstand tropic temperatures. Sadly, the end product was a hard block of candy that tasted, by the Army's own standards, little better than a boiled potato (so that soldiers would not consume them regularly). This product was very unpopular with the soldiers and not "tasty" at all, despite the ad claims. In fact, if not consumed over a long period of time, thirty minutes or more, stomach problems would result, which wartime soldiers termed "Hitler's revenge." This form of emergency ration, produced by many different candy companies and often the first thing thrown away by troops, was discontinued during the war.

Players Big and Small

Many companies chose to advertise their wartime work, and it is not surprising that the major automobile companies, for the reasons listed above, would be the largest advertisers as well. This included not just companies like Ford, General Motors, Nash, Studebaker, and Desoto, but also their subsidiaries. By far the most active was General Motors, which advertised under their own corporate name, but also those under their varied automobile name brands, primarily Oldsmobile, Cadillac, and Pontiac, as well as their other component subsidiaries, the Allison Engine Company, and Fisher Body Works. Not only did these companies have the resources to fund well-designed advertising campaigns, but they also had the most to gain, and it is for this reason that their ads can easily be found in the most popular magazines of the day. Next in line among prodigious advertisers were those manufacturing, fuel, and transportation companies that had national name recognition. This included companies like United States Steel, B. F. Goodrich, Goodyear, Western Electric, Socony-Vacuum (now Mobil), Ethyl, Quaker State, and Pennsylvania Railroad. These company's specialty items, such as steel, rubber tires, communications equipment, oil, and gasoline were not only vital components of major weapons systems, but they were also in short-supply on the home front. Beyond these big players, there were thousands of smaller companies that also advertised weapons of war in relation to their own products and war-time production. These companies had no national name recognition, though they were certainly locally or regionally well known, and perhaps even leaders in their specialty industry, and manufactured products that were not for general consumer use. This included such items as cowl fasteners (United-Carr Fastener), roller chains (Diamond Manufacturing), or self-locking

You press the button . . . it does the rest

Kodak's K-24 Aircraft Camera is completely automatic. In reconnaissance, you push a switch button on your "stick" and the camera, in the nose or tail, clicks away. In a bomber, it is in the plane's belly, connected, through complex electrical controls, with the bombsight itself. Its focal plane shutter, power operated, has speeds of 1/50, 1/450, 1/900, and "time."

It is fitted, as are most other aerial cameras, with Kodak aerial lenses, including Kodak Aero Ektars incorporating elements of Kodak's revolutionary new optical glass . . . interchangeable in a range of focal lengths and speeds for different missions. Uses Kodak Aero Films in interchangeable magazines holding 56 feet, enough for 125 pictures, 5 inches square.

K-24 Aircraft Camera, built by Kodak, *"runs its own show"*

Bombardier, at left, is hunched over his bombsight which is electrically coupled with the camera, back in the belly of the bomber, automatically taking pictures every time bombs are released. At right is a gunner covering the nose with his "fifty."

TANGLING with fighters and flak while you make a bombing run . . . or scurrying over enemy country at low altitude on a reconnaissance job . . . the last thing you have time for is "keeping a snapshot record of your trip."

Yet, in reconnaissance, that's really what you're out for—and in bombing, you want to bring back "picture information" on the relation of your falling bombs to the target . . . for the camera has the ability to make a record of details you couldn't possibly see and remember.

Pretty hopeless, without a camera that "runs its own show." Kodak's K-24 is built to do just that.

On a reconnaissance flight—with no bombs to unload—you press a button for each picture, operating the fixed-position camera by remote control. Or if you want to make a series of shots, simply hold the button down, and the camera takes 3 pictures a second.

"Chalking up the score" in the training of bombardier and pilot is another vital phase of the K-24's activity—to know how good you're getting to be, you consult the photographic evidence.

The K-24 is no hero—the men who do the flying play that role. But it does take a lot off a hero's mind.

EASTMAN KODAK COMPANY
ROCHESTER, N. Y.

REMEMBER THE PLOESTI RAID?—how at the cost of more than 500 trained fliers, our Liberators fought through one of the most heavily fortified areas in the world, to drop the bombs that knocked out one-third of Germany's oil supply?—how some of the pilots who missed the target on their first run turned back and flew through solid sheets of flame to try again? A stern example for us at home. BUY MORE WAR BONDS.

Serving human progress through photography

s du

This new U. S. seal tells you . . . **Kellogg's Rice Krispies give real wartime nutrition!**

*Delicious whole grain nourishment.** *And Rice Krispies are so* **CRISP** *you'll hear them* ***SNAP! CRACKLE! POP!***

Days crowded with war work—nights, too. Meals at all hours. Thank goodness for Kellogg's Rice Krispies! They're ready *instantly* with no fuss or bother—save time, work, fuel, and other foods.

And how good to know that such a crunchy, delicious food is one of the types recommended for daily use by the new U. S. Wartime Nutrition Program. *Rice Krispies are restored to whole grain food values in thiamin (Vitamin B_1), niacin and iron.

Serve these tempters with milk or cream—and listen to their cheery snap! crackle! pop! There's a dish to help make up for scarce protein foods and their vitamins!

Rice Krispies are oven-popped and gently toasted. Made mellow rich by Kellogg's exclusive flavor recipe. Have a package or two on hand for instant duty 'round the clock.

"Rice Krispies" is a trade mark (Reg. U. S. Pat. Off.) of Kellogg Company for its oven-popped rice.

Copr. 1943 by Kellogg Compan

ARMY'S TYPE D EMERGENCY RATION IS A CHOCOLATE BAR

There is more quick energy packed into the familiar chocolate bar than is contained in many recommended energy foods. It supplies the greatest amount of nourishment in the smallest possible bulk.

This makes chocolate an ideal food for today's fighting men who must travel long distances quickly, unencumbered by excess weight. So the U. S. Army has adopted the Chocolate Bar for its Type D Emergency Ration.

COMPARATIVE *ENERGY* VALUES

		Calories
NESTLE'S	1 5¢ Bar Nestle's Milk Chocolate	217
	1 Medium Lamb Chop (Broiled)	178
	1 Glass Milk (8 oz.)	169
	2 Eggs	140
	2 Slices Bread	200

One 5¢ bar of Nestle's Milk Chocolate gives you approximately one-tenth the minimum daily requirement for an adult in calcium, phosphorus and iron.

ON THE BATTLE FRONT the Type D Emergency Ration Bar—a chocolate bar—is sometimes the *only* food the boys carry with them. In emergencies American soldiers on every fighting front "recharge their batteries" by munching a tasty bar of this familiar energy food.

AND ON THE PRODUCTION FRONT, where the strain of long, exacting hours requires a constant refueling of human energy, Nestle's Chocolate Bars play an important role. Include a bar or two in the lunch box.

YOUNG FOLKS TOO, like the delicious flavor of Nestle's Chocolate Bars. A bar of chocolate or a dessert made with Nestle's Semi-Sweet helps restore the energy that youngsters spend so freely.

nuts (Elastic Stop). Such ads also put these companies in a spotlight, albeit a less bright one than that shone on General Motors, to not only show the public their wartime contributions, but also to perhaps induce government or manufacturing contract work for their specialty products in the future. Ads for these products, however, appeared in smaller, less-popular magazines, the ads themselves usually either smaller in size (perhaps a half or quarter page), in black and white format rather than vivid color, and often without the same high-quality graphics. Examples of such magazines that these companies utilized to get their messages out included *Popular Mechanics*, *Yachting*, *Aero Digest*, *U.S. News* (founded in 1933 and the predecessor to *U.S. News and World Report*), and countless other trade and specialty publications that did not, by far, have the same audience and advertising reach as magazines like *Life*. Indeed, unlike during World War I, when the advertisers suffered from decreased revenues, during World War II advertising was a boom business. According to the trade group Ad Age, the number of advertising agencies in the country expanded greatly, from 1,628 in 1939 to nearly 6,000 by 1948. Likewise, money spent on advertising increased from $2.1 billion in 1941 to $2.8 billion by 1945. For sure, the arsenal of democracy was big business in more ways than one.

The Artists

The advertisements created during World War II have become so iconic over the years, their artwork telling such compelling stories, that many of the men that created them during the war years have become recognized for their talents and contributions. In the past, those who have worked in advertising, either as artists or copywriters, have been described unfairly as "hacks," someone producing unoriginal art purely for commercial purposes, but for many of the advertisements created during World War II, the artists produced powerful and iconic works of art that remain relevant and relatable down to the modern day. Perhaps the most well-known of these artists was Norman Rockwell, who created many home front scenes for *The Saturday Evening Post*, including his famed Rosie the Riveter cover in April 1943. However, the Rosie the Riveter image, which is most iconic, was not an advertisement, but a factory poster created by J. Howard Miller for the Westinghouse Company in 1942. For those whose specialties involved America's weapons of war, we may mention Chicago artist Fredric Tellander, known for his Studebaker ads; James M. Sessions, whose watercolor creations depicting the jeep and other works are highly collectible and held in many institutions across the country; Dean Cornwell, an illustrator, painter, and muralist who was the predominant advertising artist of his time and the creator of many illustrations for the Fisher Body Company; Fred Ludekens, a self-trained artist and illustrator who worked for a New York City ad agency during the war and was known for his illustrations for the Nash-Kelvinator company; and Ernest Hamlin Baker, another self-taught artist who created a number of ads for U.S. Steel during the war and for years worked with *Time* magazine and illustrated many of their "Man of the Year" issues. These are just a few of the many artists who produced wartime ads whose work still endures, providing us a unique window into the past.

2

"Reading" the Popular Magazine Ads

Having discussed some of the business and strategic decisions surrounding these weapons of war ads, it is now time to take a look at their actual content. What does this information, in word and pictorial form, tell us about the war effort, and the American mindset in general from 1942–1945? Some of the themes used in these weapons ads are classic in form and timeless, something obvious that we can easily understand even in our modern world. Other aspects of these ads, however, are reflective of a different era, and their cues may be either more subtle or provocative, and thus subject to either being missed altogether, or misunderstood. Finally, we might even look at what these ads do not show or tell us—can we learn anything about the war years by what has been omitted from these advertisements? While what is discussed in this section might be viewed at first glance as merely subjective in nature, many aspects of these ads can be more clearly defined if looked at with an open eye, and with all the facts behind them clearly understood.

Words v. Pictures

The first thing that is noticeable about wartime ads in general, and especially those featuring weapons, is their high words (known as "ad copy") to picture ratio. This seems unusual to us in the modern day, where magazine print advertising, whether it be cars, clothing, or makeup, is all about the visuals, and any wording, beyond the listing of a website or store where such an item could be purchased, is very limited. However, look at many of the ads featured in this book, and you may see an ad featuring one, maybe two, visual images, accompanied by multiple paragraphs of ad copy. Indeed, some of these advertisements more resemble actual magazine articles rather than advertisements because of the large word counts in their ad copy. The structuring of ads in this manner during this time was, of course, a deliberate one, and for several reasons. First and foremost, as previously discussed, these companies were not selling products that were then available for sale, be it a Buick automobile or a washing machine, or if they were selling a particular item, such as Hanes underwear, it might be in constant short supply. While the visual images depicted what the company was doing or making to help the war effort, the large amount of ad copy was deemed necessary to completely tell the story, the gist being that, first, a given company's products would be available once the war is over and peace ensues, secondly, that a shortage of their products on the home front for now meant that they were helping, in essence to win the war, and third, American consumers should do all that they can, including buying war bonds, to support the war effort. These stories were told in countless different ways in World War II ad copy, all of them requiring a large word count. Another reason for these "wordy" advertisements, however, was also purely a result of the times. Remember, this was a time when Americans gained their information about the wider world in only several different ways, unlike today, where radio, broadcast and streamed television, the internet, and all our personal cell phone devices and their applications provide readily available information on a twenty-four-hour-a-day, seven-day-a-week basis. Not so in the

1940s, when citizens gained their information from just print media, in the form of newspapers and magazines, radio programs, as well as movie theatre pictures and newsreels to a lesser degree. Ad copy in magazines had to tell the full story, in both words and pictures, because it was the primary go to media for both public and consumer driven information.

Patriotic Symbolism

These types of images in all wartime ads are among the most common advertising themes for obvious reasons. However, for weapons-themed ads, they were not the most common. Those that did use the patriotic themes often featured such well-known American icons as Uncle Sam, one heavily used by the Pennsylvania Railroad especially, and our national bird, the bald eagle. Uncle Sam in many ads has his sleeves rolled up, symbolic of our nation's "get to work attitude" about the war, while the eagle is usually featured with a fierce countenance, sometimes at rest, but often, as in Budweiser's wartime ads, with wings outstretched while soaring in flight. Common catch-words used in these ads that reinforce patriotic and American ideals include "freedom," "destiny," "determination," "decent," "united," "pride," and "vitality."

Fighting Machines

Not surprisingly, this is the main theme portrayed in nearly every weapons ad. In describing the planes, tanks, ships, and guns built by American manufacturers, common words used to describe a weapon's overall design and capabilities include "craftsmanship," "precision," "power," "maneuverability," "flexibility," "accuracy," "dependable," "superiority," "rapidity," "confidence," as well as that most common of wartime themes, "Victory." Too, a number of descriptive phrases following several different themes were also used in conjunction with the above-mentioned words. These

Spirit of 1943!

Modern methods, modern efficiency—but the same old flaming spirit of 1776. What else could give men the *vitality* to produce tanks, guns, planes, armaments in such enormous quantities? What else could enable the railroads of America to handle millions of troops with such precision and smoothness...to haul *twice* the tonnage of war materials pre-war experts estimated them capable of... to take over the great oil and miscellaneous cargoes of coastwise shipping, and yet keep war transportation rolling smoothly? That spirit, as much as mechanical excellence and natural resources, is America's tower of strength. Its "secret weapon." Pennsylvania Railroad is proud to pay tribute to it, and to be a part of it.

PENNSYLVANIA RAILROAD
SERVING THE NATION

The 'A and Eagle'
Has Learned to Fly

Impassable roads? Mountainous territory? An urgent need to move fighting men, supplies and even jeeps by air? Our armed forces have found the answer. It is one of the thrilling new developments of the war—the use of gliders, which are now being produced in imposing numbers.

* * *

Can skilled metal workers and cabinet makers turn quickly from manufacturing refrigeration equipment to making glider parts? Yes indeed!

Our Refrigeration Division volunteered long ago to help Uncle Sam build gliders. The shops that once made equipment for ice cream and frozen food dealers the country over were revamped completely and old and new workers trained for this important enterprise.

INCIDENTALLY, *our Refrigeration Division was created many years ago as a result of experience gained in making millions of tons of ice to produce the world's most popular beer.*

Budweiser

In addition to supplying the armed forces with glider parts, gun turret parts and foodstuffs, Anheuser-Busch produces materials which go into the manufacture of: Rubber • Aluminum • Munitions • Medicines • B Complex Vitamins • Hospital Diets • Baby Foods • Bread and other Bakery products • Vitamin-fortified cattle feeds • Batteries • Paper • Soap and textiles—to name a few.

© 1943
ANHEUSER-BUSCH • • • SAINT LOUIS

include "battleworthy," or "battle proved," as well as "going to Tokyo," "Finish the Job," and "big push," these last phrases stating the implication that a given weapon would see the war right to its end with the capture of the Japanese capital. Another set of common terms were those frequently used in the "Keep 'em" ads...": "Keep 'em rolling," "Keep 'em flying," and "Keep 'em firing." This kind of phrasing not only referred to an individual weapon's capabilities and endurance, but also was a subtle message to wartime workers to keep such machines rolling off the assembly lines. Yet another common theme was that of "dish it out," meaning a weapon or one of its components, such as the famed Allison engine, that could deliver firepower and performance even in the toughest battlefield conditions. The Pullman Company, which manufactured trench mortars during the war, perhaps embodied the "dish it out theme" best when they stated in one of their ads that "The things we used to make were 'built to take it'—But what we make today must 'dish it out.'" Finally, in this type of ad, many manufacturers had their own unique descriptive phrase coined to embody their products performance: "mobile fortress" described a Chevrolet armored car, the M-18 Hellcat powered by Buick was a "lightning paced slugger," the Curtiss Helldiver packed a "pile driving punch," while the Navy patrol craft PC-487 built with Westinghouse components was "Geared to kill." Incidentally, this example of the use of the word "kill," though found from time to time in these advertisements, was not a common one, as those who designed them often came up with more descriptive and less, shall we say, stark words to describe their ultimate function.

Myth v. Reality

It should come as no surprise that none of the advertisements during the war depict a given weapon as anything less than the ultimate in performance and fighting power, no matter how they performed in real battle conditions. This was inevitable and understandable; were these weapons instead a consumer product that could be purchased, their failings would soon have become well-known and "false" ad claims wholly exposed. However, the weapons advertised in this era were not products, but instead actual components of our military power, as well as symbols of our military might, and so it was natural that they would be depicted in all their glory, no matter what the results in actual combat may have been. To do anything else would have been unpatriotic at best. Sometimes, even the best weapons were portrayed in situations where the full truth about performance would have been demoralizing to readers on the home front. Boeing, in one advertisement from 1944, featured the famed (and rightfully so) B-17 Flying Fortress and its performance during the Schweinfurt Raid on October 14, 1943. Though the ad does state that "It is not an easy task" and "Fortresses are lost of course-sometimes many of them on a single mission," it also went on to tout the fact that over the last year over 95 percent of them return safely on a single mission. The mention of this notorious raid in a wartime advertisement was a rare example of some battle details being told, but using the Schweinfurt Raid as an example of their bomber's success was far off the mark. In the course of this raid, one of the most disastrous of the war for the Allied bombing campaign, about sixty B-17s out of a total of 291 employed on the raid were lost outright, with one bomb group suffering the loss of thirteen of its sixteen aircraft in mere minutes, not due to poor performance by the bombers or their crews, but by a lack of sufficient fighter escorts and the overwhelming number of German fighters employed to combat the raid. Of course, the true results of this raid would not become more fully understood by the general public in America until after the war was over. While the B-17 was a truly remarkable aircraft, at the opposite end of the spectrum is the advertising done by the Brewster Aeronautical Company for their Brewster Buccaneer and Bermuda dive bombers. Catchy names for a dive bomber, but you say you have never heard of them? There is a good reason for this; despite Brewster's claim that the "Navy's newest dive bombers climax 23 Years of pioneering," this naval aircraft, by all accounts, was the worst airplane produced during the war and was deemed a miserable failure by every country that made it part of their air forces. Lastly, in between these two examples of great and terrible fighting aircraft, we might mention the Bell Aircraft Company and its ads for their P-39 Airacobra. It was a radically different fighter in form, had an imposing look, and was heavily armed, Bell claiming that it "will blast the biggest bomber from the sky." This, however, turned out to be the P-39's biggest failing, as the Airacobra was a very poor performer at altitude and was rejected by Britain's RAF after only one combat mission. The U.S. Army Air Force did use the P-39 in the Pacific with only moderate success, again due to poor performance. However, the Soviet Union employed the P-39 with great success against the *Luftwaffe*. Like in modern times, advertising during the war always told the best possible story, and could never tell the full story without hurting the war effort. Finally, it is also interesting that in most, but not all cases, American weapons were shown to be invincible and very seldom portrayed battle damage. One exception was advertised by the Desoto Division of the Chrysler Corporation, which made components for the B-26 Marauder bomber and depicted one in a photograph heading home with actual battle-damage, but touted its rugged construction. One of my favorite ads in this category is the accompanying one seen here for Pepsi Cola, which presents a battle-damaged truck in a more light-hearted and cartoon-like fashion. Finally, the development of the famed jeep also serves to prove that even during World War II, manufacturers' ads were not always truthful for reasons of profit and future sales. Willys-Overland was cited by the Federal Trade Commission during the war for their claim that they invented or developed the jeep on their own and was ordered to cease and desist in making such claims. The very first jeep manufacturer was actually the Bantam Car Company, and when Willys tried to claim the trademark for the jeep name as their own, the FTC denied their application (Willys would not be granted a trademark until 1950), while Willys was also sued, evidence enough that car companies knew what would be at stake in the post-war hustle to gain new customers.

270
February, 1943
NAVY'S NEWEST DIVE BOMBERS
CLIMAX 23 Years OF PIONEERING
Twenty-three years ago U. S. Marine aviators pioneered precision bombing with fighter planes aimed at the target in a dive. By 1926 the U. S. Navy was developing aircraft especially designed to withstand the unprecedented stresses imposed by this new technique. Fleet squadrons were performing regular training operations in dive bombing tactics.
Today this unrivalled background of engineering, technical development and experience has made possible the modern dive bombers now in production by Brewster and other manufacturers.
BREWSTER Blasters
BUCCANEER AND BERMUDA DIVE BOMBERS

The American G.I.

In many of these weapons-themed ads, the soldiers and sailors that manned them naturally played a large part in the narrative. In visual form, the soldier or sailor is usually portrayed in a confident and determined manner, his mind clearly focused on the job at hand of winning the war, whether he is on the move on the ground, or manning an artillery piece. In some ads, he is determined as a gritty fighter, with perhaps a five o'clock shadow or some dirt and grime on his face, but never too war-weary or with head hung low. In others, he is depicted, sometimes at rest, sometimes in the heat of battle, with a smile on his face. One of the most effective and powerful series of ads was produced by Nash-Kelvinator and gave a soldier's thoughts while in the heat of battle. One of these depicted a soldier operating a flame-thrower and thinking about the enemy that hated him, and the fact that he was "willing to fight and die" for his country, his buddies and his family back home. Soldiers' and sailors' thoughts of the home front are occasionally mentioned, with, not surprisingly, Kodak's ads being among the most appealing, one of them depicting a group of submariners reading their letters from home, stating "make your letter a real snapshot from home." It should also be noted that the men depicted are always in good physical shape, appear to be of average height or above, and are always white in skin tone. More about the issue of race will be discussed below. As to the words and ideas used to describe our soldiers and sailors, terms like "the boys" and "American boy," ones symbolic of youth, innocence, and purity, were most common, though an ad by Nash Kelvinator for a Corsair Navy fighter, calling its pilot "a lad from the USA" provided a unique alternative. Also common were the terms "fighting man," "American fighting men," "freedom's fighter," and "fighting flier," all of which spoke to both a soldier's literal job at hand, but also as a larger symbol of American might. Other terms describing the fine qualities of our "fighting men" were also common, such as "courageous crews" and "gallant flyers," while such individual words as "heroes" and "warriors" are easy to find. However, the depicting of American soldiers and sailors in these ads was not just about showing them "getting the job done," it was also about those at work on the home front who powered our arsenal of democracy and the idea of them providing a soldier "good weapons to fight with and he'll do the rest," as was stated in North American Aviation's ad for the B-25 bomber. In similar fashion, Pontiac stated in an ad for the Oerlikon 20-mm anti-aircraft guns they manufactured, "Just like them, we're giving it everything we got." One final theme in conjunction with this theme was that of wartime workers doing their job well, so that our soldiers would have "confidence" in their equipment, perhaps most starkly depicted in an ad by the Pioneer Parachute Company.

...And We'll All Stay Free!
A willingness, on the home front, to get along with less than
he customary amount of such preferred products as Utica Bodygard
Jnderwear, is making it possible for industries like ours to give to
reedom's fighting men the vital materials necessary to total victory.
'TICA KNITTING COMPANY • UTICA, N. Y. • ANNISTON, ALA.
UTICA
BODYGARD
KNIT
BUY
MORE
BONDS

SPLIT SECOND
Accuracy!
A few split-seconds ago he stepped off into five thousand feet of nothing, with only a sprinkling of cloud-fleece between him and solid unyielding earth. And yet, he is eased back to safety by the greatest sustaining force in the world . . . CONFIDENCE.
Pioneer Parachutes are designed, made and pre-tested on split second accuracy. It is an engineering and production job of which we're proud. Yes, American flyers and paratroopers have confidence in Pioneer parachutes.
PIONEER PARACHUTE COMPANY, INC.
MANCHESTER, CONNECTICUT, U. S. A.
PHONE MANCHESTER 4157
CABLE ADDRESS
PIPAR
MANCHESTER, CONN. U. S. A.
CHENEY
SILKS

Women and the War Effort

As has been well documented, World War II spurred a dramatic change in the lives of American women, many of whom were employed outside the home for the first time. Taking the place of men, they were heavily employed in wartime factories, manufacturing all kinds of goods, including munitions and weapons of war, all embodied in the ideal of Rosie the Riveter. Women also enlisted in the military beginning in early 1942, performing jobs, many of them clerical, which were previously filled by men. This included over 100,000 women in the Women's Army Corp (WACs), 86,000 as Women Accepted for Volunteer Emergency Service (WAVEs) in the Navy, as well as 19,000 in the Marine Corps Women's Reserve, and about 10,000 in the U.S. Coast Guard Women's Reserve (SPARs). Another important military role was fulfilled by those women, some 61,000 in number, who served in the Army and Navy Nurse Corps, some of whom experienced combat conditions and were taken as prisoners of war. Another group of women who were vital to the war effort were the female pilots of the civilian WASPs, Women Airforce Service Pilots, which was formally organized in 1942, though proposed previously in 1939. Once accepted into the programs, these women, who already had earned a civilian pilot license, were retrained by the Army Air Force at bases in Texas, where they operated with but little overall support. Once trained, the WASPS were employed in a number of duties, which helped free up nearly 1,000 male pilots during the war, including ferrying new aircraft from factories to air bases around the country, towing targets in the air and simulating ground strafing missions for training purposes, as well as carrying cargo all across the country. Like their male counterparts, they flew in all kinds of hazardous weather and conditions and were very versatile, flying over twenty different types of aircraft (male wartime pilots were usually only trained on several types). Thirty-eight WASPs died overall in the course of their wartime service, twenty-seven on active missions, the rest while undergoing training. Despite their services, these women were not recognized as military personnel and received no benefits or awards for their service during the war. In fact, it was not until 1977 that they were given veteran status, and in 2009, its members were awarded the Congressional Gold Medal. With these dual roles that millions of women played during the war, it is not surprising that they would be prominently featured in numerous magazine advertisements. The vast majority depicted them on the home front, either in the role of running the family household while her husband was off fighting the war, or as workers in wartime factories. Their depictions in a military setting in such advertisements were also common but limited in scope, primarily consisting of recruiting ads for the WACs or WAVEs or highlighting the service of Army nurses overseas. An example of the first-mentioned type of ad was sponsored by the Libby Glass Company of Toledo, Ohio, and is interesting in that, in typical fashion of the day, it offered a woman a chance to serve her country, and possibly provide skills for a post-war career, but also advertised the fact that "Drills and training are in keeping with women's physiques" and "Becoming Winter and Summer uniforms are furnished free." The Army nurse-themed ads were used by a number of different companies, many of which, like Douglas and Nash-Kelvinator, were producing weapons of war. Nearly all depict an attractive nurse, usually made-up complete with lipstick, and often in a battlefield or evacuation hospital setting. Though they are stereotypical images today in some aspects, they are striking in nature and would have been a real-eye opener, and surely an inspiration to future Army nurses, to those on the home front unaccustomed to seeing women in such roles in modern warfare. Finally, perhaps the most striking advertisement featuring a woman and her relationship to weapons of war, is one put out by the R. J. Reynolds Tobacco Company for their Camel cigarette brand. Its title reads "I Tame Hellcats" and features pilot Teddy Kenyon, who worked for the Grumman Aircraft Corporation beginning in 1942 to serve as a test pilot, alleviating a shortage of pilots during the first year of the war. It was a gamble by Grumman that paid off: not only did the company gain a skilled and valuable test pilot, but they featured her and two other female test pilots, Lib Hooker and Barbara Jayne, in a number of media events that gave the company good publicity. Cecil "Teddy" Kenyon (1914–1985) was a very accomplished pilot already, having gained her license in 1929 and in 1933 won the National Sportswoman's Flying Championship at Roosevelt Field in New York, using some of the prize money to buy her own plane. Even though she would not fly military planes after the end of the war, she continued to fly right up to the time of her death.

Thousands of women are needed for vital non-combatant duties with the Women's Army Auxiliary Corps, which is now serving with the Army of the United States.

It's *your* chance to serve your country in an important job here or overseas, releasing a soldier for combat duty.

You'll be proud and thrilled to be in the WAAC. There are many specialized duties open to you, and every effort is made to place WAAC members in the work they like best. Your WAAC training may fit you for a new post-war career.

The WAAC does everything possible to make military life pleasant for its members. Drills and training are in keeping with women's physiques. Becoming Winter and Summer uniforms are furnished free. WAAC pay is the same as soldiers'—$50 to $138 a month—and all medical and dental care, meals and quarters are furnished. You have full opportunity for advancement—all officers come up from the ranks.

If you are 21 to 44, between 5 and 6 feet tall, either married or single and in good health, you can enroll in the WAAC. You need only two years of high school or its equivalent.

You are needed now in the WAAC. Ask at any U. S. Army recruiting office for further information, or write to—

APPOINTMENT AND INDUCTION BRANCH
A. G. O., WASHINGTON, D. C.

Libbey

This page is published in the interest of WAAC recruiting and the cause of Victory by
LIBBEY GLASS COMPANY
Toledo, Ohio Established 1818
Makers of Libbey Safedge Glassware and Libbey Modern American Crystal

"I LOOKED INTO MY BROTHER'S FACE"

Even now, I can't sleep.

All night long the distant thunder of the guns was like the sad sound of surf along the shore at Manasquan where we spent last summer. And all night long I heard again the words I said bending over the litters as the wounded came in...

"Where are you hurt, soldier?"

Now, not even the blessed numbness we pray for in this place can keep me from living over and over again the moment when, sponging away the dark red mud, I looked into my brother's face.

He said, "Don't cry, Sis." And suddenly we were children again, playing nurse and wounded soldier on the battlefield of our yard back home, and I was crying because it seemed so real and I was scared.

I grew up last night.

Out here, I've seen my share of war. Women strafed in the streets . . . hospitals bombed . . . ripped sheets, splintered beds, the living and dead tumbled together. And I've stood it, because I'm an Army Nurse and that's my job.

But a nurse is a woman, first. And when someone you love is wounded, something breaks inside, and the war hits home.

Hits home to you . . . and to your mother and dad in the little Iowa town where you were born. Hits home to the heart of America.

And then you know why we're out here. Not for glory. Not for new worlds to conquer. Not for the sake of great, high-sounding words...

But to make sure we keep on having the kind of America my brother and I grew up in . . . to make sure we'll always have a hand and a voice in helping to make it an even better land to live in. To make sure that we'll come home to the America we've always known . . . where we can make our lives what we want them to be . . . where we'll be free to live them out in peace and kindness and security.

That's what my brother and I are fighting for. Keep it that way until we come back!

• • •

Here at Nash-Kelvinator, we're building 2,000 h.p. Pratt & Whitney engines for Navy Vought Corsair fighters . . . making intricate Hamilton Standard Propellers . . . readying production lines to build Sikorsky helicopters for the Army Air Forces . . . working day and night to make sure our sons and brothers will soon be coming home again . . . to make certain that someday soon we'll turn again to peaceful things, to the building of an even finer Kelvinator, an even greater Nash.

• • •

NASH-KELVINATOR CORPORATION

THEY GIVE THEIR LIVES, WE LEND OUR MONEY. BUY MORE WAR SAVINGS BONDS AND STAMPS!

NASH KELVINATOR

African Americans and the War Effort

As mentioned previously, by looking at these advertisements, we can tell much about the American mindset during the war. However, it is not just what we see, but what we do not see that is important as well, and something that highlights what we have always known to be true, advertising seldom tells the whole truth in general, only that which their sponsors believe the public wants to see or would be most appealing to them, no matter the actual facts. That is the very nature of advertising. Looking at all the ads in this book, and indeed through the pages of any popular magazine of the war years, you will not see any ads that feature African Americans, men and women, and highlight their contributions to the war effort, either at home as factory workers or as members of the Armed Forces at home or abroad. It is a stark omission, though not a surprising one, for both on the civilian and military fronts, whites had difficulty coming to terms with the roles African Americans could and should play in the fight for freedom in the 1940s. Of course, African Americans were fighting for freedom on two fronts—that of our country's overall freedom from Axis tyranny, yes, but closer to home, the fight for freedom from discrimination and for equal opportunity. The latter goal would not be fully achieved, of course, and the gains that were made in that fight—for black women to work in wartime factories or both black men and women to serve in the Armed forces with valor and distinction—were something that advertisers had no interest in highlighting. Why not? Because whites on the home front were uncomfortable, at best, with African Americans assuming these new roles (no matter how highly qualified), and their white counterparts as a whole did not want them in the same foxhole, on the same ship, or, more bewildering, on the assembly lines and factory floors. Historian Megan Taylor Shockley has documented this last fact in minute and painful detail in her article about Detroit's wartime manufacturing plants. Despite the fact that President Roosevelt issued Executive Order #8802 in June 1941 banning racial discrimination in the nation's defense factories, there was no mechanism for enforcement, no real punishment for offenders, and little recourse for black workers. There were many black women available and ready to work to do the job in the Detroit area: in 1943, Ford's Willow Run plant employed less than 300 black women, most in menial jobs, in their 15,000 strong female workforce. Likewise, Chrysler's main Dodge plant employed but fifty black women out of a total of 1,500 women, while GMC's Diesel plant in Detroit employed 2,000 women, none of them black. Sadly, when black women were hired, albeit in small numbers, white women went on "hate strikes" in response. As Shockley writes, "white women tried to maintain segregation on the assembly line and in restrooms and cafeterias. Strikes occurred when white women walked off production lines rather than share space with blacks.... In 1943 Chrysler and Packard were both wracked by a series of work stoppages until black women got the UAW to support their right to work." Little known or remembered incidents like these, ugly ones that hurt the war effort, are a reminder why advertisers had no reason to use black faces in wartime ads—it was these very same hate-filled white women that perused their customer's magazines in their off hours. To be fair, not all white women felt this way, but opposition to black workers was nonetheless strong and an ongoing problem throughout the war. The other reason for this lack of African American representation in advertising was the fact that there was, during the war, only one African American magazine, the *Negro Digest*, then in print, founded by the famed black businessman and publisher John Johnson (the later creator of *Ebony* and *Jet* magazines) in late 1942. This magazine, which first had a small distribution because many newsstands refused to carry it, operated on a shoe-string budget, and no major corporations spent their advertising dollars here. As a result, the images, and, by association, contributions of African Americans to the war effort would not be highlighted in advertising form by magazines that catered to white households, this being done instead by the influential black newspapers of the day, such as the *Pittsburgh Courier* and *The Chicago Defender*. As for the highlighting of black soldiers, both male and female, and sailors in wartime ads, the trials and tribulations they went through to serve in segregated units has been well-told elsewhere, and just as with black workers in the defense industry, few white Americans were interested in seeing black combatants highlighted in white magazine ads. Forget the fact that men like the Tuskegee Airmen and Navy stewards like Dorie Miller and Leonard Roy Harmon, both awarded the Navy Cross, had heroic stories to tell but were ignored, but for black women in the military, it was even worse. Some 6,500 served as WACs under segregated conditions and would not be allowed to serve overseas until late 1944, while the approximate 500 black women that served as Army nurses were restricted to segregated hospitals and, most offensively, treating German POWs, while black nurses were restricted from the Navy until the day the war in Europe ended in 1945. In all, prior to Pearl Harbor, less than 4,000 African Americans were serving in the U.S. military, but by 1945, over 1.2 million would be serving on the home front and overseas. Sadly, the stories of their service and sacrifice would remain out of public sight and never received its full measure of recognition, certainly not in national magazines, nor hardly anywhere else for that matter.

Native Americans and the War Effort

One small but interesting aspect of some of these advertisements is the cultural appropriation that was demonstrated in regards to Native Americans. Conflicts between Native Americans and whites in our country, known collectively as the American Indian Wars, had occurred since colonial times, and the war did not end until 1924, with the end of the Apache Wars in the Southwest. Because of this history, these conflicts were well-embedded in recent memory, and terms once commonly used were resurrected for use in World War II ad copy. Some of these advertisement's wording is not surprising; it was perhaps natural that the Indian Motorcycle Company would advertise that their bikes, now being used by the military, are "in warpaint today," while the famed P-51 Mustang Fighter, named after a wild horse that was widely used by Native American tribes in the Southwest like the Apaches, Navajo, Utes, and Comanches, was advertised as being "on the warpath" and was further described as having the qualities of the tribes that used them including such words as "tough," "fast," "hard-hitting," and "elusive." In addition to these specific examples, many other weapons-related ads mention such Native American related concepts as that of being "on the warpath," and "hunting grounds," this being a complete misunderstanding of their culture, as the hunting ground concept was not about killing an enemy, but rather hunting for game to feed members of the tribe. Two other aspects of some of the ads that were produced are also of note. The first of these is the fact that some employ stereotypical fictional Native American speech, sometimes called "Hollywood Injun English," as described by anthropologist Barbra A. Meek. This is amply demonstrated in an ad campaign for Western Ammunition, which depicts their production along with the faces of a white pilot and what looks to be an Indian scout, the primary copy reading "Plenty game ... you gettum soon." This type of stereotyped speech was likely influenced by the popularity of the Lone Ranger radio broadcast, which first aired in Detroit in 1933 and became so popular that it was picked up by several national radio networks, including NBC in 1942. Of course, the Lone Ranger's sidekick was a Native American, the equally famed Tonto, who spoke "Hollywood Injun." On the other hand, the ad for Boeing featuring one of their famed B-17s named *Suzy-Q*, depicts the nose art of the 93rd Bomb Squadron, featuring a caricature of a Native American warrior. Such nose art was common during the war and Native American themes were popular subject matter. Another famed bomber, the B-24 named *Squaw*, which survived the Ploesti Raid and was later sent on a war-bond tour, featured a scantily-clad Indian maiden. The name of this bomber has long been considered an offensive slur against Native American women, one that is both racist and misogynistic, but remained in common use among whites long after World War II. Of course, stereotypical images of Native Americans such as those portrayed in nose art on American bombers, were used long before the war—even the well-known and long controversial logo of baseball's Cleveland Indians, later known as Chief Wahoo, was in use by the mid-1930s. In the end, these stereotyped portrayals of Native Americans meant that they, like African Americans and Japanese Americans, received no credit in the advertisements aimed solely at white audiences, yet another factor in obscuring their contributions to the war effort. In fact, about 25,000 Native Americans served in the varied branches of the U.S. Armed Forces, about one-third of all able-bodied Native American men overall. The most prominent of these soldiers were Cpl. Ira Hayes (1923–1955), a Pima Native American from Arizona who joined the Marine Corps in 1942 and fought in the Pacific, gaining fame as one of the men that raised the American flag over Iwo Jima in February 1945, as well as the Navajo code-talkers, a group of several hundred Native Americans who spoke Navajo and English and developed their language into a military code beginning in 1942, one that was never broken by the Japanese and remained classified until 1967.

The Face of the Enemy

In some ways, this aspect of World War II advertising, defining the enemy, whether for home front goods or for our weapons of war, is the most interesting. The concepts of both identifying, or putting a face to the enemy, as well as punishing them for their misdeeds (in words as well as on the battlefield), are powerful ones that have a long history, ever since the concept of warfare emerged early in man's history. So, how were our enemies portrayed in the advertisements seen on the home front? The three Axis dictators, Hitler, Tojo, and Mussolini, sometimes appeared together, but almost always in cartoon or caricature form, with Hitler appearing in more ads than the other two. In some weapons ads, soldiers for these countries also appear, but with a difference. The German soldier, who appears less frequently in these ads than Japanese soldiers, was usually portrayed as a dark, shadowy figure, foreboding with Nazi insignia and wearing the iconic "*Stahlhelm*," the distinctive coal-scuttle helmet worn by German soldiers. Japanese soldiers, however, were often portrayed like their leader, in cartoon or caricature form, usually small in size, skinny, often with glasses, and often with a pinched, rodent-like looking face, and often on the run. How Germans were portrayed overall was different, because of America's close connection with that country historically, and the many prominent German-Americans in our country, including such men as Dwight Eisenhower. Unlike during World War I, where Americans of German descent were vilified to the extreme, President Roosevelt thought little of the idea of gathering them up in large numbers in internment camps because, after all, many of these men (like my grandfather Frederick Knoblock) were good citizens and would become good soldiers. Too, these German Americans looked like many other Americans, white in complexion, their ethnic makeup indistinguishable aside from their surname. During World War I, many families of German descent Americanized their last name, "Schmidt" becoming "Smith," and so on. While some Germans were indeed held in internment camps, their numbers were very small, maybe 300 in number, and drew very little attention. As for Japanese Americans, many of whom had lived on the West Coast for generations and were every bit as loyal to their country as any other, they suffered a much different fate. As a result of the sneak attack on Pearl Harbor, in February 1942, Roosevelt issued Executive Order 9066 ordering that Japanese Americans on the West Coast were to be confined in concentration camps during the duration of the war, their loyalty to our country heavily doubted. Those Japanese Americans living in the east were not affected, and the policy would last until late 1944, when the Supreme Court ruled that holding citizens without cause was unconstitutional. Younger Japanese workers began to be released in late 1944, but the camps were not fully closed until early 1946. During the years they were open, approximately 120,000 Japanese Americans were ripped from their homes and transported to one of ten camps in the western U.S. and forced to live in crowded and squalid conditions, while another 1,500 or so were interned in Hawaii. Racism against Asians in California and the West Coast states had a long history well before Pearl Harbor, dating back to the Gold Rush years, and was still prevalent in the years leading up to World War II, but events at Pearl Harbor, in effect, legalized this racism. Not only did Japanese Americans not look like the rest of (white) Americans, they still retained their own culture and way of life, making them prime targets. In fact, the dehumanization of Japanese soldiers in our media ads simply mirrored what was happening in real life on the home front. The words used to describe our enemies, too, went hand-in-hand with the visual images. Almost never was a German soldier described as a German, but always as a "Nazi," which catered to the idea among Roosevelt and many other Americans that the Germans were essentially good people, different than the Nazis who ruled Germany. History paints a far-murkier story of what the German people supported when it came to Nazi policies. To that end, the most foreboding symbol used in any advertisement, and then only occasionally, was the Nazi swastika. Interestingly, the German language itself was seldom referenced in wartime ads, the notable exception being that for the famed P-51 Mustang fighter by North American titled "Notiz" and giving warning to the *Luftwaffe* that the Mustang and American bombers were coming to their skies. On the other hand, the Japanese symbol of the Rising Sun, in and of itself innocuous, was seldom used. As to names bestowed on their combatants, the term "Jap" was very frequently used, with other unflattering or racist descriptors often added, including that for an iconic Willys jeep ad which refers to the enemy as the "jabbering Japs in the Solomons," in reference to their foreign and perceived incomprehensible language. In short, all of these ways in which our advertisements portrayed and described the enemy were meant to do one thing at its most basic level—dehumanize the enemy. By doing so, it not only made a justifiable war even more easy to fight, but with the rising number of dead on both sides, it made the enemy casualties more palatable; after all, these were "animals" being killed, not human beings. In fact, a number of weapons ads, not surprisingly those for rifle, ammunition, and related equipment, portrayed shooting the enemy as no different than going duck hunting or varmint shooting. One telling ad in this regard states this ideal in stark form, that for the Redfield Gunsight Corporation.

Revenge Motivation

The idea of "revenge," primarily against the Japanese, was an oft-used theme that was employed in advertising, primarily as a way to motivate wartime workers and boost the morale overall of those on the home front. This was an incredibly effective effort in print form and served as a continual reminder to Americans how the war began, and how it would end on our terms. The term "pay-off" was the most common theme for a number of these weapons manufacturers, including the PT boats made in part by Nash-Kelvinator, but by far the most appropriate was that ad by Cadillac for the P-38 Lightning fighter, titled "Pay-Off for Pearl Harbor." This ad, one of the most powerful and iconic of the war, came out in 1944, just months after revenge against the planner of the Japanese attack on Pearl Harbor, Admiral Isoroku Yamamoto, had been exacted. The mastermind of the Japanese Navy, Yamamoto, was targeted for death in Operation Vengeance in 1943, to be carried out by the Army's 13th Air Force, utilizing pilots of the 339th Fighter Squadron, 347th Fighter Group, intercepting Yamamoto on his flight from Rabaul to Bougainville in the Solomon Islands, his route determined after his flight orders were decrypted by U.S. naval intelligence. On April 18, 1943, a force of eighteen P-38 Lightning fighters were dispatched on a 1,000-mile round trip flight to intercept the plane carrying Yamamoto and shoot it down. This they did with success, suffering the loss of only one pilot who failed to return. Thus, it was that the P-38 really did exact the "Pay-off for Pearl Harbor," an event that was a great boost to American morale at home, not unlike that of the Navy Seal raid that killed Osama bin Laden in 2011 during the War in Afghanistan. Yet another Pearl Harbor-themed ad was that for the B-25 Mitchell bomber, whose manufacturer advertised the bombs it dropped as "Pearl Harbor forget-me-nots." This theme for this bomber, too, was highly appropriate, as it was sixteen B-25s, flown in the famed Doolittle Raid, which took off from the deck of the carrier *Hornet* and hit the Japanese mainland for the first time in April 1942, stunning the Japanese government and boosting morale at home just months after the Pearl Harbor disaster.

A Unique Legacy

Having discussed the many and varied aspects of these weapons-themed ads, we may wonder about their legacy. For sure, the time of World War II was a unique period in American and world history, and one of rapid technological development in all fields imaginable. America's vast industrial strength, our arsenal of democracy, was awakened by this war, with nearly every aspect of that growth publicized in our popular magazines. Just over twenty years before, America went to war with fabric and metal

"THIS IS THE PAYOFF..."

There she sits . . .

Crouched on the sea . . . big, black . . . every inch of her a battleship . . .

And every stinking inch—Jap!

We're coming in . . .

Her searchlight blinks . . . then winks full on . . . and the glare strips us down and we're running in naked and alone . . . under her five-inch guns, under her barking pom-poms . . . twelve against twenty-four hundred . . . only two hundred to one . . . so

We're coming in!

his is the payoff . . . this is the knock-t . . . this is what we were trained for . . . s is what we teamed up for . . . *this* ar!

This is the way to attack! With the tin fish running free and hot . . . and the odds so high we're madmen or demons or gods! And our enemies' hearts pump hard and their shots go wild as they realize . . .

We're coming in to win!

This is the way to fight! Not as a slave ready to die at a dictator's command . . . but as a free man fighting to live . . . fighting for the things that make life worthwhile . . . fighting for my right to dare, to pioneer, to do great things in a great spirited way, to win great victories as a *free* individual in a land where there must always be not only liberty and justice, but the freedom of opportunity that is the breath of life to me.

That's what I'm fighting for.

That's what makes this war worthwhile.

That's what I want when I come back.

. . .

Here at Nash-Kelvinator we're building Pratt & Whitney engines for the Navy's Vought Corsairs and Grumman Hellcats . . . Hamilton Standard propellers for United Nations bombers . . . governors, binoculars, parts for ships, jeeps, tanks and trucks . . . readying production lines for Sikorsky helicopters. All of us devoted to winning this war . . . to speeding the Peace when our men will come back to their jobs and homes and even better futures than they had before . . . to the day when together we'll build an even finer Kelvinator, an even greater Nash!

NASH-KELVINATOR CORPORATION
Kenosha • Milwaukee • DETROIT • Grand Rapids • Lansing

Pay-off for Pearl Harbor!

Three years ago, the sneak attack on Pearl Harbor found America unprepared to defend its rights. Yet, even at that early date, Cadillac was in its third year of building aircraft engine parts for military use. Today we look hopefully forward to the time when this important contribution to America's air power will pay off in such a scene as that illustrated above.

For more than five years we have been working toward that end. Back in 1939, we started building precision parts for Allison—America's famous liquid-cooled aircraft engine—used to power such potent fighters as the Lightning, the Warhawk, the Mustang, the Airacobra and the new Kingcobra.

In addition to our work for Allison, which has included more than 57,000,000 man-hours of precision production—we assisted Army Ordnance Engineers in designing the M-5 Light Tank and the M-8 Howitzer motor carriage, and have produced them in quantities. Both are powered by Cadillac engines, equipped with Hydra-Matic transmissions.

We are now building other weapons which utilize some of our Cadillac peacetime products. We can't talk about all of them yet—but we are confident they will prove significant additions to Allied armor.

Every Sunday Afternoon . . . GENERAL MOTORS SYMPHONY OF THE AIR—NBC Network

CADILLAC MOTOR CAR DIVISION GENERAL MOTORS CORPORATION

LET'S ALL
BACK THE ATTACK
BUY WAR BONDS

airplanes with open cockpits, horse-drawn artillery, and gas masks, but by the end of World War II we were building the most modern airplanes the world had ever seen, nearly 900-foot-long aircraft carriers, and everything in between. And nearly all of these weapons, all but the most secretive, like the atom bomb, were advertised, either directly or indirectly, in the nation's leading publications, as you will see in full in the following pages. Never before had this been done, and never since. During the Korean War, there were also advertisements that featured our weapons of war, some for companies like Sikorsky Helicopter, or Douglas Aircraft for their AD4 Skyraider. However, the vast majority of military related ads were recruitment ads for the U.S. Army and Air Force, and what was really different from the previous war were the lack of advertisements for companies like General Motors or Kelvinator. These companies were no longer on a war-footing, and would no longer be producing weapons or their components for the war effort since the mobilization required to do so was far, far less massive than during World War II. The same holds true for the Vietnam War, but with an added twist. Now that television was ensconced in American society and media by the 1960s, this became the go-to place for recruitment advertising, though these still appeared in print form early on, but less so as the war grew in unpopularity. The era of World War II was, indeed, a period of time where our country and all levels of society were, for over four years, totally immersed in the war in all aspects of our lives in a way that has not been experienced since. That is what makes these advertisements, ordinary artifacts from everyday life, so compelling. What follows is a concise listing of America's weapons of war, separated by category. For each entry, general information about that weapon's production, performance, and usefulness during the war is discussed in brief, accompanied by an iconic wartime advertisement in which it is featured. The information about these planes, aircraft, armored vehicles, and other weapons is necessarily brief and does not cover in full their technological details or the many variants that came out about as the war progressed. Further detailed information about their development and technical specifications can be found in the source bibliography, as well as in numerous online databases. This work only covers those major weapons that were widely used by American forces, with only a few notable exceptions, and I have not included ads for weapons deemed as obsolete, those that were built solely under the Lend-Lease program and never used by American forces, or those that were not built in significant numbers and never saw combat before the war ended. This includes such machines as the Vought SB2U Vindicator torpedo bomber and the Marmon-Herrington CTLS light tank (both obsolete), the M22 Light Tank and Martin Baltimore bomber (Lend-Lease), as well as the M6 heavy tank, Grumman F7F Tigercat, and Bell P-59 Airacomet jet, all of which were latecomers to the war.

Part II

WEAPONS OF WAR IN THE MAGAZINE PAGES

3

Tanks and Other Armored Vehicles

The ads for these types of weapons are among the best conceived and boldest of all the weapons ads, this being for the simple reason that the companies that built them were the largest and most important automobile companies in the country, while many of their components, such as engines and transmissions, were also built by large and well-known heavy equipment manufacturers, including John Deere, Caterpillar, and Mack Truck. These were companies that had the expertise to convert quickly to manufacturing tank components, as well as the resources to fund expensive wartime advertising campaigns. Altogether, their production and expertise were invaluable to the war effort, these companies together manufacturing just over 108,000 tanks and self-propelled guns during the entire war. Nearly 25 percent of all tanks were built at one factory, the Detroit Arsenal Tank Plant in Warren, Michigan. Though built and operated by Chrysler beginning in 1940, this plant was a government owned facility, and continued to produce tanks for the U.S. military until its closure in 1996. The other big producer, as the ads in this section clearly show, was GMC's Cadillac Division, whose armored ads are some of the finest of the wartime era.

M5 Stuart Tank

This light tank, named after Confederate General J. E. B. Stuart, was used throughout the war both by U.S. forces as well as being supplied via Lend-Lease to Britain and other Commonwealth nations. Several versions of this tank saw service, including the pre-war M3 version and the improved M5. The older version used a radial engine, but these were in high demand for use in aircraft, so the improved M5 used twin V-8 Cadillac automobile engines with a pair of their new Hydramatic transmissions. The Stuart was armed with a 37-mm gun and three .30-cal. Browning machine guns but was considered to be lacking in firepower. The M3 Stuart first saw combat action in North Africa with British forces and though comparable in power to Axis tanks, fared poorly primarily because the German's *Afrika Korps* was much better trained, though many design flaws also became apparent. Later on, the British would use the Stuart primarily as a reconnaissance tank and tried to avoid direct tank *v.* tank action. The Stuart's role in U.S. armored forces declined after the defeat at Kasserine Pass in early 1943, though it saw its greatest success at the Battle of Anzio in early 1944, helping to break through German beachhead defenses, but thereafter was relegated to a secondary role as the M24 tank came into wider use. Still, the Stuart remained in use throughout the entire war, with nearly 23,000 built between 1941 and 1944, about 9,000 of them the improved M5 version. The Stuart was known for being fast, able to reach 36 mph, and had an operation range of about 100 miles on its 89-gallon tank. Weighing in at about 33,500 lb. and nearly 16 feet in length, it carried a crew of four men, a driver, assistant driver, gunner, and the tank commander. Cadillac was not the tank's only producer; Massey-Harris and the American Car and Foundry Company also built Stuarts, while the famed Mack Trucks company manufactured their heavy duty transmissions.

Some go Through – Some go Over !

Under the direction, and with the coopera-tion, of Army Ordnance—Cadillac has de-veloped, and is building, what have proved to be two of the most effective pieces of armament in the Arsenal of Democracy.

One is the M-5 Light Tank—a fast, quick, highly-maneuverable weapon, armed with a high velocity, 37 mm. cannon. This tough, speedy, hard-hitting tank is one of America's great "surprise weapons"—ideal for upsetting enemy formations. Like a speedy halfback, it darts through the slightest opening in the line, or "runs the ends," as the need may be. It is almost as fast as a motor car.

The other is the M-8 mounting the Army's 75 mm. Howitzer cannon. Utilizing the same chassis as the M-5, it gives to demolition artillery a degree of mobility it has never known before. With this weapon, big guns can follow their targets—keep the position from which they can do the most good.

The two units that give these weapons their power and maneuverability were developed by Cadillac in peacetime: the Cadillac V-type engine and the Hydra-Matic transmission.

The quickness with which these peacetime units were sent to war not only attests their inborn quality of design and construction—but it indicates the splendid manner in which Army Ordnance has utilized the nation's resources to astound the world with its armament program.

CADILLAC MOTOR CAR DIVISION — GENERAL MOTORS CORPORATION

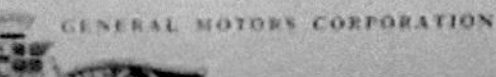

LET'S ALL
BACK THE ATTACK
BUY WAR BONDS

Army M-3 tank, "land battleship" of America's modern mechanized army. Armed with cannon and machine guns.

The Army had to have a trans-mission—one capable of con-verting the speed of a 400 h.p. airplane engine into the smashing force of a 30-ton tank. ***Mack is building it*** —a mighty 8,000 pound gearbox, the largest ever manufactured in quantity production—more than 300 times the weight of a passenger car transmission.

The largest trucks in Army service are gigantic six-wheel Macks. Great fleets of Mack dumpers are clearing the way for air-base construction at defense outposts. Mack skill and re-sources contribute in more than a score of ways to America's military might.

The Tough Jobs Go to Mack!

MACK TRUCKS, INC., NEW YORK, N. Y.

MAKERS OF WORLD-FAMOUS GASOLINE AND DIESEL-POWERED TRUCKS, BUSES, FIRE APPARATUS AND MARINE ENGINES

7

M4 Sherman Tank

This medium tank was the most important and widely-used tank among all Allied nations during the war. Some 50,000 Shermans were built during the war, this number exceeded only by the Soviet T-34 tank, and it led many an Allied offensive after 1942. Weighing up to 84,000 pounds depending on the variant, the Sherman was 20 feet long and stood 9 feet tall, carrying a crew of five—the commander, gunner, loader, driver, and assistant driver/loader. Its main gun was a 75-mm, though some carried a 76-mm or a 105-mm howitzer, as well as a .50-cal. Browning machine gun and two .30-cal. Brownings. Its maximum speed was 30 mph in optimal conditions, its engine being built by either Chrysler, Ford, Continental, or Caterpillar. The Sherman first saw action with the British at El Alamein in North Africa in 1942 and was very successful, so much so that many believe the U.S. Army was complacent with the design and did not encourage further development. Whatever the reason, by 1944 the Sherman was inferior to German tanks, lacking sufficient firepower and protective armor. Many Shermans, when struck by enemy shells, caught fire easily and exploded, and thus gained the grim nicknames "Tommycooker," by British crews, or "Ronson" (after the famed cigarette lighter) by American crews, for their tendency to burn. This deathly problem was later determined to be caused by the stowage practices of the tank's 75-mm ammunition, as well as a problem with those tanks powered by gasoline engines as opposed to diesel versions. Even later in the war, when the Sherman was clearly outclassed, it prevailed in battle due to their overwhelming superiority in numbers *versus* the Germans. The Sherman was also aided by an incredibly effective system developed by U.S. armored forces for reclaiming and repairing battle-damaged tanks and getting them back into service quickly. Despite its flaws and lag in development, the fact that it was easy to manufacture and fought in nearly every major action in the war makes the Sherman one of the most important weapons that resulted in victory for the Allies. Further, the tank's versatile chassis resulted in many variants; there were Shermans equipped with bulldozers, a small number of Jumbo Shermans equipped with very thick armor, as well as those equipped with rockets and Zippo flamethrowers. The Sherman was manufactured at a cost of about $45,000 per tank by ten different makers, Cadillac being a prime contributor, during the war, and afterwards was the Army's main tank until it was phased out in 1957.

M24 Chaffee Tank

Named after U.S. Army General Adna Chaffee, Jr., who was a key driver in tank use and development during the war, this light tank was developed as a result of the shortcomings of the Stuart tank. It came into service in 1944, being produced by Cadillac and Massey-Harris, and weighed 40,500 lb. The Chaffee measured 18 feet long and was manned by a crew of five. The tank was sent overseas to France in November 1944 and saw its first major action in December at the Battle of the Bulge. Since it came about late in the war, only about 4,700 were built and the M24 had little effect on the outcome. However, it was generally well received, being fast, powered by two Cadillac engines, and armed well with a 75-mm gun, though it was criticized for being very lightly armored, it being vulnerable to every German tank. The Chaffee continued to serve in the U.S. Army until after the Korean War, when it was replaced.

Howitzer Motor Carriage M8

This tank-like appearing armored vehicle was actually a self-propelled howitzer gun, mounted on the same chassis used by the M5 Stuart. The M8 was used primarily by medium tank battalions in Europe beginning in 1942 and assigned to assault troops of cavalry reconnaissance squadrons to provide close support against fortified enemy positions. Because the high-powered 75-mm gun (later changed to 105-mm late in the war) could be greatly elevated, it was very useful in taking out hillside emplacements. It was not designed, despite its appearance, to fight tanks. However, like the Stuart tank, the M8 had a crew of four, was powered by twin Cadillac engines, and because it was lightly armored, it could reach the speed of 35 mph. In all, 1,778 were produced, all of them by Cadillac.

M18 Hellcat Tank Destroyer

What looks like a tank, has the firepower of a tank, but is not actually a tank? That would be the M18 Hellcat, which was the ultimate in development for the tank destroyer class of armored weapons during World War II. The concept of a tank destroyer was simple: it had to be fast and pack a punch, which the Hellcat did, being capable of speeds up to 50 mph, and armed with a powerful 76-mm gun, the same as the Sherman tank. However, the role of a tank destroyer was not to fight one on one with an enemy tank out in the open, but rather more in an ambush type of role and as direct fire support for infantry units. The armor for the M18 was thin and could be penetrated by any enemy shells, though this same problem plagued every American tank by 1944, but this light armor meant it could travel quickly to its destination, outflanking enemy armor aiming for the same point. The cockpit of the M18 was also open in design, unlike a tank, which provided for great visibility, though its crews were left vulnerable to enemy fire and shell fragments. The Hellcat was preceded by tank destroyers operating on the chassis of the M3 Stuart tank, but this made them too heavy and too slow. Thus, an entire new chassis was designed by Buick for this ultimate tank killer and, interestingly, was tested on the same course as Buick's peacetime automobiles were, designed to achieve a high speed, but also capable of fording 6 feet of water, climbing over walls, and smashing through small buildings if need be. Production of the M18 began in 1943, 2,500 produced overall during the war, all by Buick, at a cost of about $55,000 each. The M18 saw action in both the European and Pacific theatres, but saw the most action in Europe, where it achieved the highest kill-to-loss ratio of any armored vehicle at the time after first being deployed during the Battle of Anzio. The M18 subsequently saw heavy action in Northern Italy, France, and Germany. It often bested the feared German Panther tank and achieved outstanding success at the Battle of the Bulge, where four M18s of the 705th Tank Destroyer Battalion, along with the 1st Battalion of the 506th Parachute Infantry Regiment, destroyed about thirty German tanks, some of them heavy Tigers, near Noville. Among the many units to deploy the M18 Hellcat was the 827th Tank Destroyer Battalion, 12th Armored Division, a segregated unit of African American soldiers. Despite its combat inexperience, this battalion's Company B destroyed fifteen German tanks in action around Rittershoffen in January 1945.

M3 Half-Track Armored Personnel Carrier

Over 60,000 units of this iconic type of armored vehicle were constructed during the war, most of them of the M3 design. They were used by every Allied army and on every front of the war, being used, as their name suggests, to move armored infantry personnel quickly during armored offensives. Though widely used, they were unpopular amongst troops at first because of their open topped design and small amount of armored side protection, leaving them vulnerable to artillery shells from above and machine-gun fire on the ground. It is for this reason that they gained the nickname "Purple Heart boxes." Its other major flaw was that the rear tracks sometimes broke on rough terrain, but a fix was soon found for this flaw and by and large these cars were rugged and dependable carriers. The M3, derived from the older M2, was built by Diamond T, White Motor Company, and Autocar and was powered by a White 147-hp engine, capable of speeds of up to 45 mph. Early versions had a mount for a .50-cal. machine gun just behind the front seats, while later models had a distinctive raised "pulpit" mount for the machinegun, as well as side-mounted .30-cal. machine guns. The windshield, of course, was bulletproof, while the distinctive front grill had armored shutters to protect the radiator. There were many variants of the half-track, including those armed with antiaircraft guns and self-propelled guns, as well the M5, which was manufactured by International Harvester under largely the same specifications because the manufacturers of the M3 could not keep up with demand.

Armored Car

This is another iconic vehicle of the war, of which several types were built by U.S. manufacturers. The U.S. Army version was the M8 armored car built by Ford Motor Company. It was produced between 1943 and 1945, its numbers totaling just over 12,000 of all types. Ironically, in its many ads, Ford does not seem to have advertised this vehicle, or if they did, not very prominently. On the other hand, their peacetime competitor, Chevrolet, also built an armored car in their factory for use by British and Commonwealth forces and acquired via Lend-Lease. This was the T17E1 Staghound, of which some 4,100 were built, 250 of them by Ford early on under the name Deerhound. The Staghound was similar to the American M8,

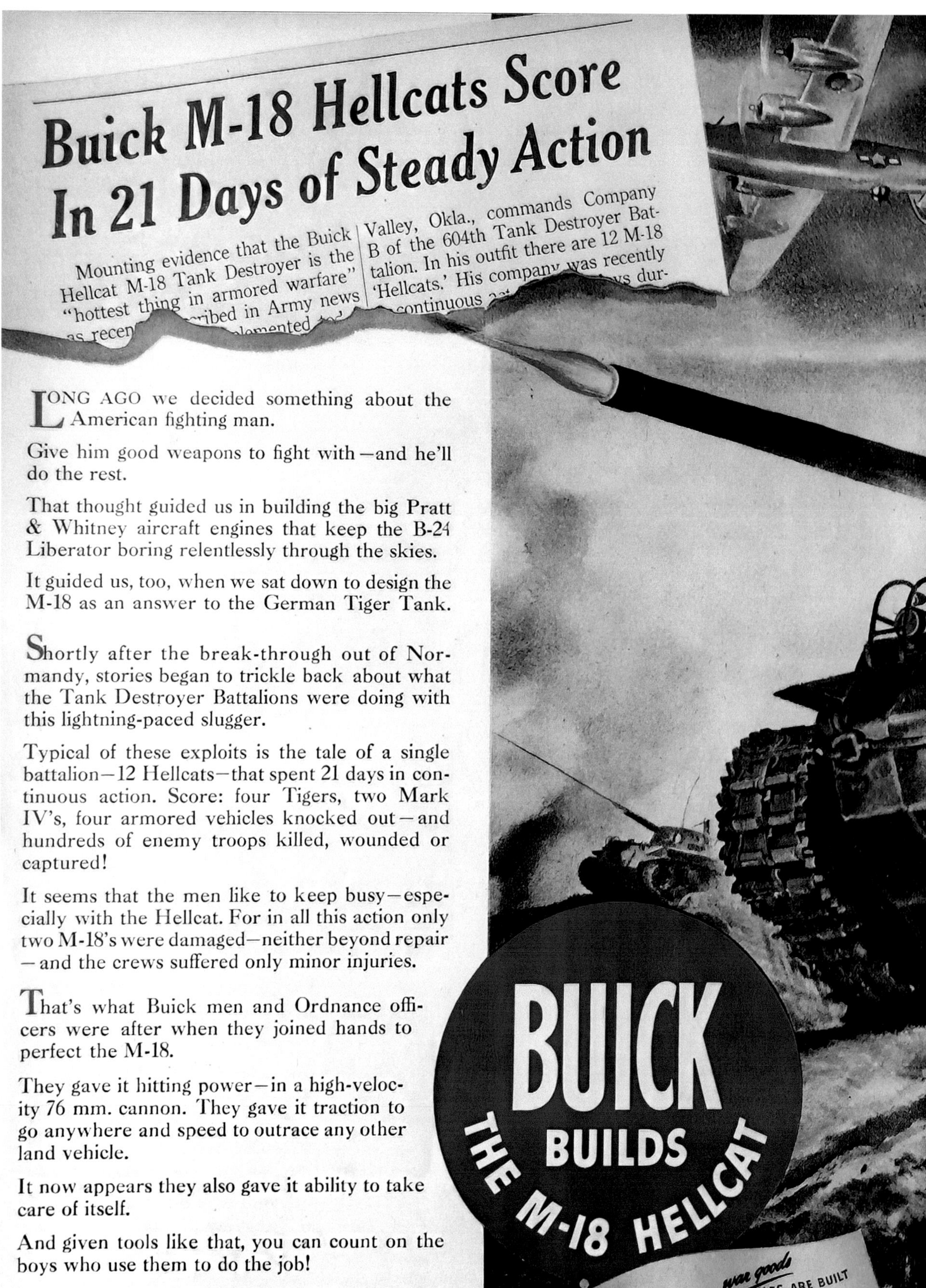
Buick M-18 Hellcats Score In 21 Days of Steady Action
Mounting evidence that the Buick Hellcat M-18 Tank Destroyer is the "hottest thing in armored warfare"
Valley, Okla., commands Company B of the 604th Tank Destroyer Battalion. In his outfit there are 12 M-18 'Hellcats.' His company was recently
LONG AGO we decided something about the American fighting man.
Give him good weapons to fight with—and he'll do the rest.
That thought guided us in building the big Pratt & Whitney aircraft engines that keep the B-24 Liberator boring relentlessly through the skies.
It guided us, too, when we sat down to design the M-18 as an answer to the German Tiger Tank.
Shortly after the break-through out of Normandy, stories began to trickle back about what the Tank Destroyer Battalions were doing with this lightning-paced slugger.
Typical of these exploits is the tale of a single battalion—12 Hellcats—that spent 21 days in continuous action. Score: four Tigers, two Mark IV's, four armored vehicles knocked out—and hundreds of enemy troops killed, wounded or captured!
It seems that the men like to keep busy—especially with the Hellcat. For in all this action only two M-18's were damaged—neither beyond repair—and the crews suffered only minor injuries.
That's what Buick men and Ordnance officers were after when they joined hands to perfect the M-18.
They gave it hitting power—in a high-velocity 76 mm. cannon. They gave it traction to go anywhere and speed to outrace any other land vehicle.
It now appears they also gave it ability to take care of itself.
And given tools like that, you can count on the boys who use them to do the job!
Every Sunday Afternoon—GENERAL MOTORS SYMPHONY OF THE AIR—NBC Network
BUICK BUILDS THE M-18 HELLCAT
WHEN BETTER war goods ARE BUILT BUICK WILL BUILD THEM

BUICK
POWERS
THE LIBERATOR
BUICK DIVISION OF GENERAL MOTORS
YOU LEND A HAND WHEN YOU LEND YOUR DOLLARS
INVEST IN MORE WAR BONDS

STRAFER
BEWARE!
WHEN the Half-Track raises its umbrella of ack-ack fire, there's trouble above for the strafer . . . as there is trouble below for tanks that rumble within range of its mighty 75. . . . Fighting on all fronts, Half-Tracks by Autocar are upholding the performance expected of this famous name. Yet they are only one of the mobile units rolling out of Ardmore for our Army, Navy, Marine Corps, and Air Forces. . . . Stand by for better *trucks* to come. Keep your pledge to the U. S. Truck Conservation Corps.
AUTOCAR
MANUFACTURED IN ARDMORE, PA.
SERVICED BY
FACTORY BRANCHES FROM COAST TO COAST
Buy More Bonds for Victory

Now it can be told!
Meet One of the Allies' Secret Weapons
THE CHEVROLET-BUILT ARMORED CA
Instrument of Victory Extraordinary
This new armored car is unique among wheeled vehicles
this war . . . a fourteen-ton roving weapon—with th
speed of a passenger car, the firepower of
tank and the armor of a mobile fortres
BUY WAR BON
AND KEEP TH
A trainload of Chevrolet-built armored cars bound for Europe. The British call them "Staghounds" because they're fast and maneuverable, and their "jettison" gas tanks give them a 500-mile range without refueling.
CHEVROLET DIVISION OF GENERAL MOTORS

except that it was far more heavily armored and thus weighed much more. Both were armed with 37-mm guns and capable of reaching speeds up to 55 mph, the British car slightly longer and with a crew of five as opposed to four for the M8. Armored cars like this were not designed as offensive weapons, but rather in a reconnaissance role, being equipped with radio communications to report on enemy movements and ever-changing battle situations. The Staghound first saw service in the Italian campaign, the car's large size making it unsuitable for narrow city streets, but after the fall of Rome and the greater mobility of Allied forces moving on, was a better performer, primarily serving in armored regiments, being used at both the headquarters and squadron level.

M3A1 Scout Car

This vehicle was the primary contribution to the war effort by the White Motor Company of Cleveland, Ohio, which built 21,000 of them between 1939 and 1944. This 4×4 "car," which weighed in at just over 5½ tons, was powered by a Hercules JXD six-cylinder motor and was capable of reaching speeds of up to 50 mph. It was typically armed with one or two Browning .50-cal. Machine guns. The car's side armor was made by the Diebold Lock and Safe Company, but the vehicle was of an open-top design, having only a canvass top when required by weather. The car was popular with crews and it was primarily employed first in armored units as both a reconnaissance and command vehicle, having a crew of two and capable of carrying six passengers. The M3A1, however, was a poor off-road performer, which sometimes gave the army headaches. This scout car only saw combat action in Europe, over half of the scout cars produced going to American allies under Lend-Lease, including nearly 7,000 to the British, who called it the "White Scout Car" and 3,300 to the Soviet Union. Despite its large numbers, the M3A1 began to be phased out in 1943, replaced with the M8 armored car, but the scout car remained in wide use in rear areas and for escorting military convoys. Interestingly, a modified M3A1 scout car was personally used by General George Patton, having extra armored protection and a raised rear fighting compartment. A picture of an actual M3A1 can be seen in the dedication portion of this book.

4

Navy, Coast Guard, and Merchant Marine Vessels

Advertisements for naval and related vessels during World War II were produced under different circumstances than those of most other types of main weapons systems. Unlike Navy and Army Air Force airplanes, armored vehicles, and many types of guns, these ships were built by either government owned shipyards, like the Norfolk Naval Shipyard and the Navy Yards at Portsmouth, New Hampshire, and Mare Island, California, or shipbuilding companies, like Bethlehem Steel or Bath Iron Works, with longstanding relations to the U.S. Navy. These companies had no real need to advertise their contributions to the war effort as they had nothing to sell to the general public and largely depended on government contracts. One major exception was the Electric Boat Company of Groton, Connecticut; this premier builder of submarines before, during, and after the war down to this day, was a private company that competed with the government owned submarine yards in Portsmouth and Mare Island and was not averse to advertising the submarines that they built. Because of these overall circumstances, most of the ads featuring the largest vessels were produced by smaller companies who manufactured some of their components, while smaller vessels like PT boats were advertised by those companies that actually built them.

Aircraft Carriers

At the beginning of the war, the fact that airpower would soon reign supreme over the old-fashioned battleship had yet to be fully realized by the U.S. Navy. When the war began, the Navy only had seven aircraft carriers, but the attack on Pearl Harbor changed that when an aggressive shipbuilding program was put into place. By the end of the war, the U.S. had built twenty-four large fleet carriers (CVs), nine light carriers (CVLs), and approximately 108 escort carriers (CVEs). This represented a remarkable achievement that was unparalleled in naval history, for it is these carriers, beginning with their action at the Battle of the Coral Sea in May 1942, followed by the decisive and tide-turning victory at the Battle of Midway in June 1942, which would lead the way to victory in the Pacific war. The most notable of the carriers built during the war were those twenty-two in the *Essex*-class, they displacing 27,000 tons, manned by a crew of 2,900 men, and carrying up to 100 aircraft. Famous examples of this renowned class include USS *Yorktown*, USS *Lexington*, and USS *Intrepid*, all of which are now museum ships. The light carriers (CVLs) too did their part, with the nine that were built averaging 11,000 tons displacement, manned with a crew of 1,400 men, and carrying forty-five aircraft. The most numerous class of carriers built, however, were the escort carriers (CVEs), which are represented in the ad shown here. These were built in great numbers by private shipyards like Ingalls and Kaiser Shipbuilding, and though designed as carriers, they were completed in short order based on the mass production techniques that were used to build Liberty ships. As their name implies, escort carriers, often called "jeep carriers" for their small size, were put on convoy duty in the Atlantic and the Pacific to provide air cover for vulnerable merchant ships, but were also heavily used during amphibious operations in the Pacific. The most numerous of these

Fine 18" x 15" full-color enlargement of this painting sent on request while supply lasts. Write for Lithograph M to Electric Boat Co., P O Box 69, New York 3, N. Y., enclosing 10c for postage and handling.

Trustworthy Craftsmanship

The sleek hull of an EBCo submarine is crammed with myriad parts and mechanisms on whose soundness and unfailing performance depend the lives of all on board. During long weeks of undersea patrols in hazardous enemy waters, EBCo's integrity, engineering skill and precision craftsmanship become vital realities to every member of a submarine's crew. Knowing this, Electric Boat has kept trustworthiness *of product a firm tradition for 45 years in war and peace.*

BUY WAR BONDS

CONNING THE *Kill*

A mighty U. S. submarine goes in for a better view of her victim. A moment ago she sent her torpedoes lashing into the flanks of another enemy warship, adding one more irreparable loss to the dwindling Jap fleet.

The Japs hate our submarines, and fear them; and no wonder! Submarine sinkings now total well over 1000! In the historic naval engagement during our invasion of the Philippines, U. S. submarines first made contact with the enemy fleet. Big Jap cruisers and a carrier were their part of the kill. After the battle, the communiqués paid special tribute to the work of the subs. In fact, a high naval official has recently said that "The submarines deserve the lion's share of the credit for knocking the props from under Japan's conquest."

With the help of the Navy, Electric Boat Company developed U.S. submarines from the crude early models of 1900 to the present big, efficient, long-range ships. And Electric Boat Company now builds more submarines than any other shipbuilder in the United States.

EBCo SUBMARINES

ELECTRIC BOAT COMPANY

33 Pine Street, New York 5, N. Y.

Electric Motors	*Submarines*	*Motor Torpedo Boats*
ELECTRO DYNAMIC WORKS	NEW LONDON SHIP AND ENGINE WORKS	ELCO NAVAL DIVISION

carriers, those of the *Casablanca* and *Bogue*-class, displaced about 7,800 tons and carried a crew of 650–800 men and could carry up to twenty-four aircraft. Many of these escort carriers, some 39 in number, were acquired by the British Royal Navy and designated as *Attacker*-class escorts, including at least five built by Ingalls Shipbuilding. Notable examples of the jeep carriers include that of USS *Guadalcanal*, which under the command of Captain Daniel Gallery caused the loss of four German U-boats. The *Guadalcanal*'s aircraft sank *U-544* off the Azores on her first cruise, on her second cruise the carrier's planes sank *U-68* and caused the loss of *U-515*, and on her third cruise she captured intact the *U-505*, now on display at the Museum of Science and Industry in Chicago, this being the first time since the War of 1812 that the U.S. Navy had captured an enemy ship at sea.

Battleships

Though the day of the battleship had passed, the large and majestic battleships would still have a part to play in World War II, primarily as gigantic bombardment platforms, as well as providing protection in large carrier task force groups. At the beginning of the war, the U.S. Navy had fourteen battleships, some of them older vessels (built as far back as 1912), seven of which were damaged or sunk in the Japanese attack on Battleship Row at Pearl Harbor. Eight new battleships would be built during the war, including the famed USS *Iowa*, USS *New Jersey*, USS *Alabama*, USS *Massachusetts*, USS *Alabama*, USS *Wisconsin*, USS *Missouri*, and USS *South Dakota*. Incredibly, all of these ships, except the *South Dakota*, survive as museum ships today, while the *New Jersey* and the *Iowa* (the lead ship of her class) have the distinction of having served into the 1990s. This class of ships was expensive indeed, and far less cost-effective than the *Essex*-class carriers, with the *South Dakota* class ships costing $77 million apiece to build. The ships of the *Iowa*-class were massive in size, displacing 45,000 tons, being 890 feet long, carrying a complement of 2,700 men, and armed with nine 16-inch guns, three each in two forward turrets, and three in one rear turret, providing massive firepower. The ad from Western Electric highlighting their communications systems and though it mentions the battleship USS *Wisconsin*, actually depicts USS *South Dakota* during her first combat action of the war in the Battle of the Santa Cruz Islands in October 1942.

Cruisers

These ships, along with destroyers, were very much the workhorses amongst the capital ships of any task force group during World War II, but were very seldom featured in any advertisements. The U.S. Navy possessed just over thirty cruisers before the war, divided evenly between the heavy and light cruiser classes, and during the war would build another forty-three, thirty-one of them light cruisers and twelve heavies. Similar to battleships, a cruiser's guns were configured in two forward turrets and one or two rear turrets, with three guns in each. The heavy cruisers, ships like the famed USS *San Francisco*, USS *Portland*, or USS *Indianapolis*, displaced about 10,000 tons and carried 8-inch guns in three turrets, while the light cruisers, which displaced

about 6,000 tons, had for their firepower twelve 5- or 6-inch guns in four turrets. Cruisers saw their heaviest action in the Solomon Islands campaign and the fight for Guadalcanal, with three of them, USS *Vincennes*, USS *Quincy*, and USS *Astoria* lost in one action, the Battle of Savo Island in August 1942. Further significant cruiser action took place in the Naval Battle of Guadalcanal in November 1942, when Task Group flagship USS *San Francisco* engaged a Japanese force and took a pounding but survived the fight, though her commander, Captain Cassin Young, as well as Rear Admiral Daniel Callaghan, were killed in action during the night battle. Other cruisers of this task group were not so fortunate; the light cruiser USS *Atlanta* was hit by an enemy torpedo and eventually sank, but not before she was battered by friendly fire from the *San Francisco*, while the light cruiser USS *Juneau* was sunk by a Japanese submarine with the loss of the five Sullivan brothers. Sadly, it was also a cruiser, the heavy USS *Indianapolis*, that was lost at the end of the war in a tragic manner. After having delivered the components for the atomic bomb, including enriched uranium, to Tinian Island on a secret mission, the cruiser subsequently departed Guam for the Philippines and was torpedoed on July 30, 1945. Of her 1,195-man crew, only 314 survived, many of them dying in shark-infested waters while awaiting a rescue that would not occur for several days. The loss of the *Indianapolis* remains the greatest single loss in U.S. Navy history. This interesting ad from Budweiser depicting an unnamed cruiser highlights the ammunition hoist mechanisms made by one its subsidiary companies.

The Ammunition is being passed

There's no monkey-business about the way the ammunition is being passed in this war, either. For example, the Navy's 5-inch 38 caliber gun throws shells at planes or surface craft at a terrific rate. Its powder and shells must come to the gun in a steady stream. How is it done? With an ingenious hoist whose tolerances are so close that the mechanism is comparable to the movement of a fine watch.

* * *

Ammunition hoists for the Navy are being produced so fast and efficiently by the Busch-Sulzer Bros. Diesel Engine Company that the organization has been awarded a second star in its Navy E pennant. Busch-Sulzer, which made engines for submarines in the last war, was founded by Adolphus Busch, the founder of Anheuser-Busch. He was the first to build Diesels in America—and the first American-made Diesel went into the Home of Budweiser. Now as then, the quest for better methods and facilities to produce the world's most popular beer never ceases.

Budweiser

In addition to supplying the armed forces with glider parts, gun turret parts and foodstuffs, Anheuser-Busch provides materials which go into the manufacture of: Rubber • Aluminum • Munitions Medicines • B Complex Vitamins • Hospital Diets • Baby Foods • Bread and other Bakery products Vitamin-fortified cattle feeds • Batteries • Paper • Soap and textiles — to name a few.

© 1943
ANHEUSER-BUSCH • • • SAINT LOUIS

Destroyers

These small but important ships, called "tin cans" by the sailors that manned them (because of their thin armor and because they bobbed in the water like a tin can in heavy weather), were not only one of the Navy's most important fighting ships, but with over 200 of them built during the war, offered shining proof of America's industrial might. Destroyers displaced somewhere between 1,600 and 2,400 tons, the larger versions, consisting of the *Gearing* and *Allen M. Sumner*-class that comprised the bulk of the destroyers built during the war and carried a crew of between 250 and 350 men. For their size, they were heavily armed with between four and six 5-inch guns and between four and sixteen 40-mm Bofors guns, as well as ten to twelve 20-mm Oerlikon anti-aircraft guns. Destroyers were also equipped with between five and ten torpedo tubes. This heavy armament, combined with top speeds approaching 37 knots, made destroyers a tough customer to deal with as they were excellent at providing anti-aircraft cover, detecting and killing submarines, as well as providing good firepower in fast moving engagements. The tin cans were engaged in every aspect of American naval operations during the war, and even before, with the destroyer USS *Reuben James* sunk by *U-552* off Iceland while performing convoy escort duty in October 1941. Perhaps the premier destroyer action of the war occurred in October 1944 during the Battle off Samar in the Philippines, when the three destroyers and one destroyer escort of the task unit Taffy 3 counterattacked against a greatly superior Japanese fleet consisting of battleships, heavy and light cruisers, and eleven destroyers. Though the destroyers USS *Johnson* and USS *Hoel*, as well as the destroyer escort USS *Samuel B. Roberts*, were sunk in the battle, with the destroyer USS *Heerman* damaged, their brave and heroic actions in attacking and inflicting great damage to the Japanese ships, causing the loss of two of them, was the stuff of which legends were made and Medals of Honor awarded. Even the Japanese could not help but acknowledge the gallant efforts by these ships, with a Japanese destroyer captain saluting the sinking USS *Johnston* as he sailed close-by to survey the scene. The destroyers built during the war were largely constructed by private shipyards, including four different Bethlehem Steel shipyards, Maine's Bath Iron Works, the Federal Shipbuilding & Dry Dock Company, and several others, though some were built at the Navy shipyards in Charleston, Boston, and Puget Sound. The ad shown here from Union Asbestos highlights the insulation used on the boiler systems of naval vessels supplied by the company.

Destroyer Escorts

This class of warships were very much like the destroyers they were named after, but smaller in size and therefore armed with smaller guns. Over 650 destroyer escorts were built during the war, manned by both Navy and Coast Guard crews, and they performed many of the duties that regular destroyers did. However, as their name suggests, their main duty was to serve as escort ships for supply and troop convoys, and did so in both the Atlantic and Pacific theatres. These vessels carried a crew of about 220 men, displaced somewhere between 1,150 and 1,450 tons, and were generally armed with three 3-inch guns, or two 5-inch guns, along with six or eight anti-aircraft batteries and three torpedo tubes. Though smaller in size and with less powerful guns than a destroyer, as well as a slower top speed ranging from 20–28 knots, they were very maneuverable and excellent at convoy protection and anti-submarine work. The destroyer escorts also served in other roles, some converted to high-speed troop transports, but others, like the gallant USS *Samuel B. Roberts* serving in Taffy 3 task group during the Battle off Samar (see above), also served with regular naval task forces. Nine of these ships were lost during the war, including the Coast Guard-manned USS *Leopold* sunk by a German U-boat, USS *Shelton*, sunk by a Japanese submarine while serving in an escort carrier task force, and the last U.S. Navy vessel lost in the Battle of the Atlantic, USS *Frederick C. Davis*, sunk by a German U-boat while escorting a convoy in the western Atlantic. This ad features USS *Bunch* built by the Defoe Shipbuilding Company of Bay City, Michigan, and the unusual method in which it was constructed. This DE was converted to a transport and took part in the invasion of Okinawa in 1945, shooting down an enemy bomber, destroying a Japanese suicide boat, and served as the flagship for a transport ship task group. The ship was subsequently decommissioned in 1946 and finally scrapped in 1965.

Submarines

One of the most important, and dangerous, branches of our military during the war was the Navy's Submarine Force. It was this elite group that not only strangled the Japanese supply line in the Pacific, but also, in conjunction with the Navy's surface fleet, harassed the warships of the Imperial Japanese Navy and sent many of them to Davy Jones' Locker. This included

750 Ton Flapjack!

HISTORY was made when the destroyer escort, U.S.S. *Bunch*, was "roiled over" successfully at the Defoe Shipbuilding yards at Bay City, Michigan. For this was the first time a steel-welded ship more than 300 feet long and weighing over 700 tons had been built upside down.

The same engineering feat that made it possible to build the U.S.S. *Bunch* in record time is producing an ever increasing fleet of sister ships—many of which are already in service on the high seas.

Defoe's unique "flapjack trick" with ocean-going warships does away with conventional ship scaffolding and allows workers to stand over their job at all times. Defoe construction methods deliver *twice the production per man hour* resulting in *double the number of ships* built at *half the labor cost per vessel.*

Resourcefulness in developing new methods and shortcuts to speed delivery of ships to the Navy is typical of Defoe engineering tradition. And when our fighting men and their allies have dealt a knockout to the Axis, the same competitive spirit, skilled workmanship and "know how" that are now setting records in producing for Victory, will be reflected in even greater values of Defoe products to serve peacetime America.

> *"Next to our immediate task of building warships faster and faster, the first responsibility of Defoe is to plan for post-war operation that will provide the maximum of gainful employment."*
>
> HARRY J. DEFOE
> Founder Defoe Shipbuilding Co.

* * *

BACK THE ATTACK — BUY WAR BONDS

Defoe workers take more than 10% of their pay in War Bonds

DEFOE SHIPBUILDING COMPANY, BAY CITY, MICHIGAN

Two White Star Renewal Citations now decorate the Navy "E" Award won by Defoe workers.

Ships for Victory
Servants for Peace

large ships like the 65,000-ton carrier *Shinano*, sunk by USS *Archerfish* (the largest vessel ever sunk by a U.S. submarine) to small patrol boats, and every type of warship in between. The average submarine, or fleet boat, displaced about 1,500 tons and was just over 300 feet long, manned by a crew of about seventy-five men. In addition to their primary weapon, ten torpedo tubes (six in the bow, four in the stern), they also carried a 3-inch deck gun and several 20-mm anti-aircraft guns if forced to fight on the surface, though this was not their intended role as the hull of a submarine was particularly vulnerable. Their primary role was to operate underwater in stealthy conditions, sneaking up to within a firing range of 4,500–9,000 yards. The closer a submarine could get to her target, the better the results, but the closer they got meant more risk in being detected and counterattacked. U.S. submarines were stationed at Pearl Harbor in the Pacific, with additional bases in Australia at Perth and Brisbane, as well as Midway Island, and typically departed on war patrols that might last only a few weeks, but usually closer to sixty days and as many as eighty days. Submarines usually worked a general area in conjunction with other boats to attack enemy shipping, but also worked in concert with surface naval ships during offensive operations. In addition, submarines also undertook special missions to land commandos on enemy-held islands, evacuate American citizens and military personnel, even evacuating the gold from the national bank when the Philippines fell to the Japanese, for which the members of the crew of USS *Trout* received the Army's Silver Star Medal, and also rescued downed fliers at sea. Submarine operations were so important that their activities by most tallies accounted for the destruction of just over 50 percent of all Japanese naval and merchant ships during the war, even though submarines made up less than 5 percent of U.S. naval forces. Their success, however, came at a high price; fifty-two submarines were lost during the war, with over 3,500 crewmen. This fact is sometimes alluded to, at least in part, in World War II magazine advertisements like the one shown here, where the phrase "Take 'er down" was used. This was the command typically given by a submarine commander when his boat was ready to make a dive beneath the waves. It was also this same command that was given by Commander Howard Gilmore as he lay wounded on the deck of his boat, USS *Growler*. He was attacking a Japanese convoy in February 1943 when he was wounded by machine-gun fire after ramming a Japanese patrol boat. Knowing his boat needed to submerge quickly to survive, Gilmore ordered the bridge cleared while he himself remained up top. When his executive officer made it down below, he waited for Gilmore to follow but instead heard the order to "Take her down." Gilmore knew he had to sacrifice his life, and that of another man left on deck, to quickly save his command. He was posthumously awarded the Medal of Honor for his actions. Sadly, Gilmore was not the only submarine hero to be killed in action; there was the hard-hitting Dudley Morton, destroyer of twenty-seven enemy ships in USS *Wahoo* (sunk with all hands in La Perouse Strait October 1943), and Samuel Dealey in USS *Harder*, known for his expertise in "killing" Japanese destroyers (sunk with all hand in October 1944 off Luzon). However, many others survived to tell their tale, including Richard H. O'Kane, commander of USS *Tang*, the top-scoring submarine of the war in the Pacific both in terms of total tonnage and number of ships sunk. He ended the war in a Japanese POW camp, one of nine survivors when his boat was sunk by a circular run of her own torpedo off the coast of China in October 1944. Just under 200 submarines that made war patrols were built during the war, both in commercial and government-owned naval shipyards, but Electric Boat of Groton, Connecticut, was the only major advertiser for submarines built by the private yards and built more submarines than any other shipyard. Two other private yards built submarines in small numbers, including William Cramp & Sons of Pennsylvania, as well as those built by the Manitowoc Shipbuilding Company of Manitowoc, Wisconsin. The other submarines were built at the Portsmouth Naval Shipyard in New Hampshire, as well as the Mare Island Shipyard in California, with the Portsmouth yard running a close second to Electric Boat for the number of submarines built, and all three yards equal (along with Manitowoc) in terms of quality, reliability, and performance.

Minesweepers

This kind of naval vessel and the men who served aboard them are some of the unsung heroes of the war. They were employed in both the Pacific and Atlantic, as well as in the Mediterranean Sea and, as their name implies, were used to clear enemy laid mines in strategic waterways and in coastal and port areas. The job was a dangerous one, with the risk that the minesweeper itself could be damaged or sunk by a stray mine that went undetected. The minesweeper used a mechanical sweep that projected from the side of the ship, which was designed to cut the mooring cables of the mines. Most

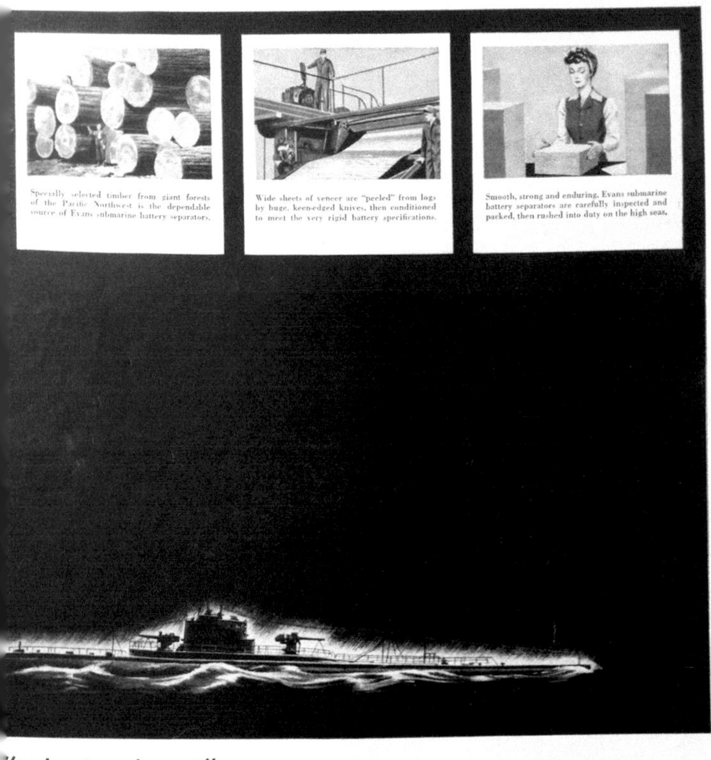

interesting is the fact that, because mines were magnetic and designed to go off when a metal-hulled vessel came in close proximity, the hull of a minesweeper was made of wood, as is shown in the accompanying advertisement. The Navy had built two types of minesweepers; the large fleet-type minesweepers included the *Auk*-class ships and those of the *Admirable*-class. These ships displaced 890 and 625 tons, respectively, and were 180–215 feet in length, carrying crews of about 120 men. Approximately 168 of these fleet ships were built during the war, all by private shipyards. The second type of minesweeper used were the small coastal or "yard" minesweepers, which measured but 215 tons and were about 136 feet in length. Over 200 vessels of this type were built, they being so small they were not even given names, but rather the letters "YMS" for yard minesweeper, followed by a numerical designation based on their sequence of building. No matter what their size, these ships contributed in all aspects of the naval war, and wherever an amphibious landing took place, whether it be at Sicily, Anzio, or Okinawa, they were there to clear the way. They also, like larger warships, suffered their share of casualties; the *Admirable*-class sweeper USS *Salute* was mined and sank while doing her duty during the invasion of Borneo in June 1945, while *YMS-30* was mined and sunk off Anzio and *YMS-481* was sunk by Japanese shore-batteries off Borneo. Of the largest *Auk*-class of sweepers, eight were lost, most due to direct enemy action, including USS *Sentinel*, which earned two battle stars for her service until being bombed and sunk by German aircraft off Licata, Sicily, in July 1943, and USS *Tide*, which was mined and sank on the Cardonet Banks off the French coast just one day after D-Day in June 1944. The ad shown here depicts the wooden hull of a yard minesweeper, along with a contact mine, an explosion being set off when an unsuspecting ship brushes up against one of the protuberances known as "horns."

Submarine Chasers

These craft, which received only the letter designation PC, followed by a number, were employed, as their name implies, in anti-submarine work, largely in coastal waters. Measuring in at just under 300 tons and carrying a crew of about eighty men, they packed a punch for their size, armed with a 3-inch gun as well as a 40-mm Bofors and five 20-mm anti-aircraft guns. Over 250 vessels of all types, some even made of wood, were built, some transferred to Allied forces, many serving in the U.S. Navy in many different theatres. Approximately six of this class of ship were lost during the war, the most notable being *PC-1261*, which took part in the D-Day operations of June 6, 1944 and was the first ship sunk on D-Day, hit by German shore batteries while leading the first wave of landing craft on Utah Beach, suffering the loss of half her crew. Other losses include *PC-558*, sunk by a German U-boat off Sicily in 1944, just after having destroyed a one-man mini-submarine, and *PC-1129*, sunk off Luzon, Philippines, in January 1945 after being rammed by a Japanese suicide boat. This Westinghouse ad details the exploits of *PC-487*, launched in February 1942 and damaged in June 1943 off Shemya Island in the Aleutians when she intentionally rammed and sank the Japanese submarine *I-24*, her captain awarded the Navy Cross while three crewmen earned the Silver Star. The ship survived the war and was decommissioned in 1947, later sold to Venezuela in 1960.

Motor Torpedo Boats

The exploits of these small but hard-hitting and daring craft are the stuff which legends were made of and, despite their small size, they gained a large amount of publicity during the war both in terms of magazine articles and magazine advertisements. Designated as PTs, or Patrol Torpedo boats, these craft had no name, but merely a number, but this does not seem to have hurt their legacy; many Americans know the

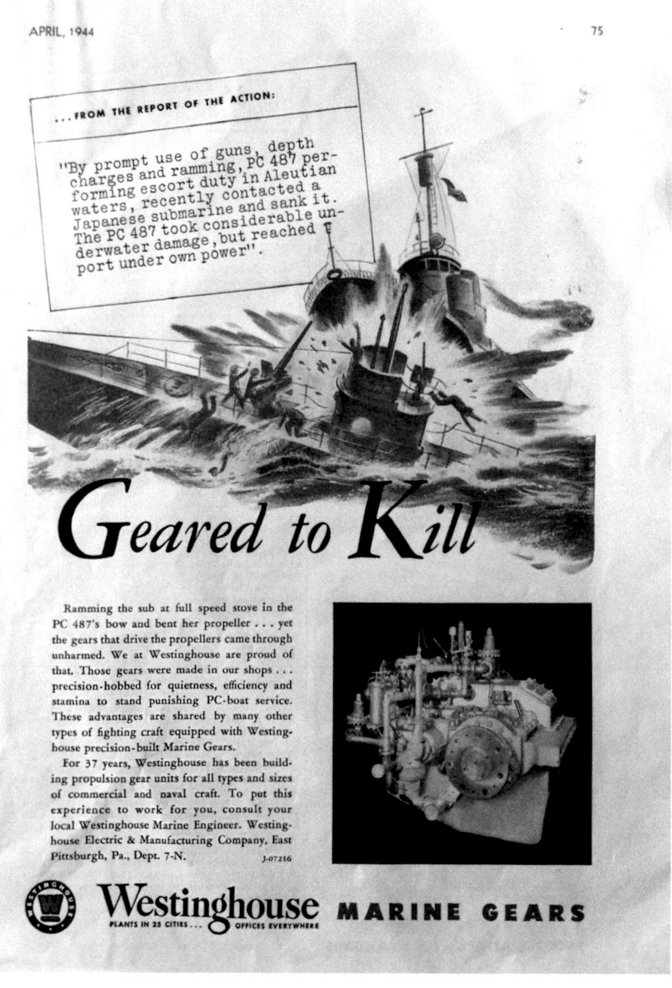

story of *PT-109*, the PT boat commanded by future president, John F. Kennedy. Some 531 PT boats were built during the war, including 326 by Elco and 199 by Higgins. Though often called "plywood" boats, PTs were actually constructed out of two layers of mahogany wood, with fabric layered in between, and were good sea boats which first saw service in the cold Aleutian Islands. These tiny boats were powered by three Packard V-12 liquid cooled engines powered by high-octane aviation fuel, and carried a twelve- to seventeen-man crew. They were heavily armed, the standard boat carrying up to four torpedoes, and protected by several 20-mm Oerlikon cannons, and at least two .50-cal. machine guns. However, there were many variants and one-offs, as PT boat commanders were very adept at procuring whatever other weapons they could find. As a result, some PT boats, like *PT-109*, carried a 37-mm anti-tank gun, while others carried rocket or mortar launchers. Whatever the case, PT boats packed a punch and were essential to winning the war in the Pacific. Ninety-nine of them were lost during the war to enemy action, while a further thirty-two were lost by friendly fire. In addition to *PT-109*, other famed PT boats include *PT-41*, which carried General MacArthur away from the Philippines in 1942, and *PT-373*, which carried him back to Manilla in March 1945, therefore helping him to fulfill his promise that "I shall return." Interestingly, after the war, the Navy had no use for PT boats and, not being worth the cost of transporting back to the U.S., a great many were piled up on Pacific beaches and burned, though fourteen survive today. This ad from Elco highlights the role PT boats played in destroying Japanese cargo barges during the fight for Guadalcanal. In their efforts to supply their troops, and later to evacuate them, the Japanese deployed self-propelled and armored barges that could operate in shallow waters, where U.S. destroyers could not go, but the small PT boats could. In July and August 1943, PT boats disrupted Japanese supply operations by sinking about two dozen of these barges, and damaged about another three dozen.

Landing Ship-Tank (LST)

Another ship type known simply by its letter designation and a number, the LST was one of a number of important specially designed vessels used in amphibious landings in theatres throughout the world. As their name implies, these beasts carried tanks to a landing beach, but also a great deal of other vehicles, cargo, and landing troops, and even reconnaissance aircraft. About 1,000 were built, displacing about 4,100 tons when fully loaded and capable of a maximum speed of 12 knots. Most importantly, they were designed with a flat keel and their propellers and rudder were given protection, all of these features enabling them to coast right up on the beach. LSTs were crewed by up to 120 men and were heavily armed, carrying a 76-mm gun, six 40-mm Bofors, and ten other types of machine guns. About forty LSTs were lost during the war, including *LST-313*, sunk by German aircraft off Gela, Sicily, in July 1943, and *LST-460*, *LST-472*, *LST-738*, *LST-749*, and *LST-750*, all sunk by kamikaze attacks in the Philippines in December 1944. The ad for Stewart-Warner shown here highlights the engine gauge components they supplied to the Navy.

Landing Craft-Infantry (LCI)

This specialty ship was used in amphibious operations, designed to carry infantry troops ashore. They displaced about 390 tons fully loaded and measured 158 feet long, powered by two diesel engines capable of reaching speeds of up to 16 knots. Able to carry up to 210 troops ashore, LCIs were armed with four 20-mm Oerlikon cannons for nominal protection and carried a crew of at least thirty men, sometimes many more depending on how they were being used. Over 900 of this type of ship were built, and they gave invaluable service, even if their image in the movies is a bit tarnished, they are often portrayed as carrying groups of seasick and retching soldiers anxious to get off and onto land. In addition to landing troops, some LCIs were reconfigured as gunboats heavily armed with rocket launchers, flagships, and some being larger in size and designated as LCI(L)s. The Maxim Silencer Company of Hartford, Connecticut, was owned by Hiram Maxim, who invented the first gun silencer and later, during World War II, produced engine exhaust silencers for naval vessels.

Landing Craft-Tank (LCT)

The LCT was a smaller landing ship designed to carry a tank to a beachhead, first designed by the British Royal Navy, and later adopted by the U.S. Navy. Over 1,400 were built between 1942 and 1944, of several different types, measuring about 285 tons, 119 feet long, powered by three marine diesel engines and manned by a crew of thirteen. They carried several 20-mm Oerlikon guns and were primarily used in the North African and Italian campaigns in Europe, as well as during the Normandy invasion, but also saw service in the Pacific. Approximately seventy of these ships were lost during the war, including *LCT-593*, *LCT-597*, *LCT-612*, *LCT-703*, and *LCT-777*, all mined and sunk off the Normandy beachhead on D-Day, June 6, 1944. This ad highlights the General Motors diesel engines supplied for LCTs and other landing craft.

Landing Craft, Vehicle, Personnel (LCVP-Higgins Boat)

The famed Higgins boat, despite its small size, was an important and versatile vessel, cheap, easy to build, and considered by many a key weapon that helped the Allies win the war. Some 24,000 of the Higgins boats were built, all in New Orleans by the company founded by Andrew Higgins. These boats were made of plywood and had a diesel engine capable of 225 hp. As its official designation implies, this boat carried troops, up to thirty-six at a time, to a beachhead, or a jeep and a lesser number of troops or other cargo if needed. They were manned by a crew of four, including a coxswain, engineer, a bowman, and a sternman. For protection, the Higgins boat was armed with several .30-cal. Browning machine guns. Because they were made of wood, they could be built cheaply, although their wood construction also meant that they had no armored protection to offer. Ironically, the Higgins boat was first used by the Royal Navy, but was eventually adopted by the U.S. Navy in 1942. The Higgins Company, because it was a private shipyard, whose products were originally designed to be used in southern swamps and marshes, advertised their contribution to the war effort quite heavily, helping to make the Higgins boat a household name.

OFFICIALLY, her name is "LST." That's Navy talk for "tank landing ship." Her job is invasion.

She's a long-geared gal of 327 feet and weighs 5500 tons beachside. At sea, she looks like a half-finished cargo ship. But when she rubs her nose on an enemy shoreline and opens her mouth—that's all, brother!

Out come hundreds of tons of hard-hitting tanks. Or hundreds of fighting men. Or jeeps. Or trucks. Or supplies. Then, like a well-bred lady, she shuts her mouth after she's had her say, and demurely sets out for another secret rendezvous.

Already, she has kissed the shores of Africa, Sicily, Italy, the Aleutians and South Pacific islands. Where she goes next she won't tell, but her date-book is filled for the duration.

This trouble-laden lady had to be sure of herself to do her job on time. Before the eyes of her engineer are instruments that tell him all he needs to know. Some of them, like the Oil Pressure Gauge, Tachometer, Ammeter and Temperature Gauges, most likely were made by Stewart-Warner. It's a privilege to have them there.

* * *

You've got to earn your rating to come aboard an LST . . . an AVR or any other Navy craft. That's why we're mighty proud Stewart-Warner instruments sail the seven seas. Into each device goes all the skilled craftsmanship that has distinguished Stewart-Warner instruments through the years. Tomorrow, this same precision and care, plus many important advancements learned in war will add new and greater meaning to the statement "Instruments by Stewart-Warner."

Many a youngster, now helping to make history, got his first "sea legs" behind a peacetime Stewart-Warner Marine Instrument Panel. Typical is "The Admiral"—adaptable for either gasoline or diesel marine engines. Today the "kin" of "The Admiral" are serving ships of war. After Victory they will again be found serving the needs of the mariners of America on peaceful waters.

INSTRUMENTS BY
STEWART-WARNER CORPORATION
CHICAGO ILLINOIS

LCM (Landing Craft Mechanized) 50 ft.

LCI (Landing Craft Infantry) 157 ft.

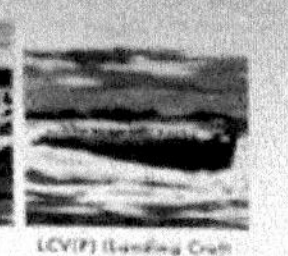

LCT (Landing Craft Tanks) 105 ft.

LCV(P) (Landing Craft Vehicle Personnel) 36 ft.

America's Fighters move in-with GM DIESELS

IN the face of enemy fire these remarkable invasion boats nose in on enemy shores and pour out America's tough fighters and fighting equipment.

They move on split-second orders—must get in and out again by themselves—on the dot, come hell or high water.

It's the kind of service that calls for utmost reliability, maneuverability and quick response.

In these capable craft—from the 36-foot LCV(P) to the big 328-foot LST—you find the engines America and our Allies know so well, General Motors Diesels.

To these engines are assigned the jobs that call for the greatest dependability the engine world knows.

AFRICA! SOLOMONS!! CHANNEL RAIDS!!! ATTU!!!!

"These Higgins boats are so tough they land directly on rocky beaches, unload troops, tanks and equipment dry-shod, retrieving themselves by their own power. They're plenty fast in assault, can turn on a dime to zig-zag away from trouble, and I never saw one capsize."

HIGGINS BOATS designed and built for the United Nations were described thus by veterans of Guadalcanal and Africa, who also said, in official records, that these boats were the "Best in the World." This praise comes from men who manned them under fire—from men whose lives often depended upon these boats' unusual maneuverability, stamina and trouble-free operation.

Today Higgins plants are engaged the clock around in manufacturing boats, planes and other products to meet the swiftly changing needs of nations at war. It is this ability to change—to pioneer—to anticipate tomorrow's needs—that makes "Higgins" a name to watch when the war is won.

Higgins
INDUSTRIES INCORPORATED
NEW ORLEANS
HUB OF THE AMERICAS

BOATS • ENGINES • AIRPLANES • WOOD ALLOYS

Treasury-Class Coast Guard Cutters

Advertisements for Coast Guard-constructed warships during World War II are very rare, for the simple fact that none of that service's fighting cutters were built during the war years. The most famed of their fighting ships were those of the *Treasury*-class, built in the mid-1930s. These ships were invaluable in the fight against the German U-boats in the Battle for the Atlantic and are considered the best class of ships ever built by the Coast Guard, some remaining in service as late as 1988. Known as "the 327s" because of their overall length, these cutters displaced 2,216 tons and were capable of speeds up to 20 knots. They were heavily armed, too, carrying two 5-inch deck guns, as well as eight machine guns and several others. They were a tough foe to deal with and served on northern convoy runs to Iceland and elsewhere, working to ward off U-boat attacks and rescue crews of stricken merchant ships when needed. While one of this class of ships, the USCGC *Hamilton*, was sunk by a German U-boat, the other six survived the war, with USCGC *Campbell* serving with distinction, sinking one U-boat by depth charge attack, and then *U-606*, previously damaged by the Polish destroyer *Burza*, after first ramming her, and then dropping depth charges and bringing all her guns to bear on the wounded vessel while escorting Convoy ON-166 from Britain to the United States in February 1943. This accompanying ad, though it does not identify any particular Coast Guard ship, clearly shows the gun crew of a fighting cutter, the men at their battle-stations awaiting the time when they can engage an enemy submarine. This ad for Pneumatic highlights the packaging and bottling equipment which was their specialty, but also, in the fine print, their manufacture of wartime ordnance equipment.

Liberty Ships

There is probably not a more famous type of ship built during the war years than the famed Liberty ships. While many might consider these mere merchant ships, not "weapons" as such, they would be incorrect. The job of a Liberty ship was to transport war cargoes around the world and, quite simply, without these cargoes, the war could not have been fought or won. Add to that the fact that Liberty ships served in war zones all around the world, and that many were lost in combat situations, and it is hard not to view them as anything but a "weapon." A total 2,710 of these standardized ships were built during the war, with 225 of them converted for use as troopships. They were built at eighteen shipyards on both coasts, and were turned out so fast that, at their peak of building, three ships were turned out every two days. The standard Liberty ship was 441 feet long, displaced 14,245 tons, was powered by two oil-fired boilers, could reach a speed of 12 knots, and carried about 11,000 tons of cargo. These ships were manned by a crew of anywhere from thirty-eight to sixty men, depending on the type, and also carried a Navy Armed Guard crew consisting of anywhere from twenty-one to forty men. Its main protection was a stern-mounted 102-mm deck gun, though machine guns were also carried. The Liberties served not just as regular cargo ships, but also as colliers, tankers, as well as tank and crated aircraft carriers. Much has been written about these ships, including their innovation and building defects, but the Liberty ships were the symbol of American industrial might, and though not known for their beauty, these ships were indeed vital to the war effort and about 200 were lost during the conflict. Notable Liberty ships include SS *Booker T. Washington*, an integrated ship captained by African American Hugh Mulzak, whose second and third officers, and chief engineer were also African Americans, and SS *Stephen Hopkins*, the only American merchant ship to sink an enemy surface ship, doing so in September 1942 when she battled the German raider *Stier*. This ad for the optic giant Bausch & Lomb highlights the Liberty ship named after one of their founders, launched in 1943, and subsequently sold to a private company in 1947.

Victory Ships

This class of standardized merchant ships were the successor to the Liberty ships, being a more modern version of the original pre-war design adopted by the U.S. Maritime Commission. The Victory ships, of which 534 were built in six different shipyards, including Todd Shipyards, were larger, being 455 feet long and displacing 15,200 tons, and were capable of a greater speed, 15–17 knots, making them better able to elude enemy submarines. They were designed so that the hull fractures that plagued the Liberty ships were solved, and with more efficient engines, they had a longer range. They were also true fighting ships, being much more heavily armed. The first ship, SS *United Victory*, came off the line in February 1944. All the Victory ships serving the United States had the word "Victory" as

With galley well-stocked below . . .

COAST GUARD GOES INTO ACTION

Coast Guardsmen are a
ed lot. They have to be — to patrol the ocean
seacoast with the tireless keenness of a fish
x. Placing depth bombs, exploding mines,
hing for subs are all in the day's duty.

ach men need plenty of hearty, wholesome food
itomatically packaged by accurate machines to
d flavor, crispness, and nourishing goodness
ist the swift ravages of damp salt air. Such
itials are double-wrapped packages of cereal,
-wrapped pancake flour, tea and crackers in
ages with moisture-proof lining . . . bottled
>, mayonnaise, mustard, ketchup, and other scientifically prepared and packaged products. And in the emergency cabinet, as well, medicines properly packaged by reliable bottling equipment.

Throughout the food and medicinal fields — as in every industry where products are packaged and bottled — Pneumatic machines are delivering the goods with unequalled precision and speed. This is one more convincing proof that Pneumatic equipment has maintained its top-ranking position because it is more soundly engineered and more accurately machined.

• • •

With nearly all of its facilities devoted to the manufacture of ordnance equipment and the remainder to the building of packaging machines which the Government considers essential, everything Pneumatic makes contributes directly to the war effort.

PNEUMATIC SCALE CORPORATION, LTD.
72 Newport Avenue, North Quincy, Mass.
New York Chicago San Francisco Los Angeles

HENRY LOMB, *from his meager pay as a Civil War captain, provided funds that helped John J. Bausch to keep alive their infant partnership. It was this partnership that became the scientific institution that supplied gun-fire control instruments for the Spanish-American War . . . that during World War I freed America from dependence upon foreign sources for optical glass . . . and is able in this war to produce record quantities of gun-fire control instruments, binoculars, flyers' goggles, aerial photographic lenses, industrial optical equipment and other precision tools of war.*

The newly-commissioned S.S. Henry Lomb. A full color reproduction of this painting, by Lt. Comm. Anton Otto Fischer, sent free on request.

To Gallant Ships and the Men Who Sail Them

The S. S. Henry Lomb is just one ship of a vast fleet that flies the proud flag of the United States Merchant Marine. She is named after Captain Henry Lomb, Civil War soldier and co-founder of Bausch & Lomb Optical Company. To those who know of this great American, this gallant ship is a symbol and an inspiration.

The spirit that will guide her along perilous convoy routes, where sleek destroyers dance alert attendance and thundering planes hover protectingly, will be his spirit of militant loyalty to duty and country . . . to prosaic jobs that must be done and done well, without thought or fear of danger.

There are few songs to these brave gray ships or to the men in oil-stained dungarees who man them . . . the men who listen and wait for the crash of enemy torpedoes. These are the ships that carry the food, fuel, ammunition and weapons . . . often the vital optical instruments of war which Bausch & Lomb manufactures.

These are the ships and men who are welcomed by no cheering throngs . . . only by the clank and groan of heavily-laden winches working in grim urgency. These are the ships and men of the United States Merchant Marine.

ESTABLISHED 1853

part of their name, while those built under Lend-Lease for Britain or Canada used "Fort" and "Park." Over 100 Victory ships were converted to attack transport vessels and, like the Liberties, the Victory ships sailed all around the world transporting cargoes in the last year and a half of the war. Many would continue to serve in years to come, as late as the Vietnam War. Like the Liberties, the Victories also saw their share of combat. Two of the converted Victories, USS *Hinsdale* and USS *La Grange*, were damaged by kamikaze attacks in 1945, with the later ship attacked in the last kamikaze attack of the war, suffering twenty-one killed and eighty-nine wounded, while SS *Canada Victory*, SS *Hobbs Victory*, and SS *Logan Victory* were sunk by a kamikaze attack off Okinawa in April 1945. Perhaps the most tragic loss was that of SS *Quinault Victory* at Port Chicago, California, on July 17, 1944. While loading a cargo of ammunition, the ship exploded, blowing the *Quinault Victory* out of the water and on to land 500 feet away upside down, while the neighboring Liberty ship SS *E.A. Bryan*, also loading ammunition, was vaporized. The accident, now called the Port Chicago Disaster, resulted in 320 men killed, many of them African American Navy stevedores, the survivors subsequently refusing to continue loading ammunition in a so-called "mutiny" due to the unsafe conditions in which they were working.

The Merchant Marine

Advertisements for the Merchant Marine Service in general are rather uncommon, though some larger shipping companies did advertise the service of their own captains and crewmen, as well as their own ships that were turned over for wartime use. The accompanying ad for the prominent Grace Line is an excellent example of a firm consumed by the war effort out of necessity, but looking to future patronage after the war had ended and regular shipping and passenger trades would resume. Were the ships of the Grace Line, and others, though, truly weapons of war? Well, that question has its origins in the long trials and tribulations of the Merchant Marine Service as a whole and their role as combatants. The fact of the matter is that merchant mariners served aboard transports and cargo vessels in every theatre of the war and many died while serving their country in countless warzones from the North Atlantic, the Mediterranean, the South Pacific, and the Indian Ocean. Merchant mariners did not just serve aboard Liberty and Victory ships, but also aboard Navy vessels and regular shipping company ships whose vital cargoes were also essential to the war effort. Despite this fact, merchant mariners, perhaps due to the death of President Roosevelt (who greatly recognized their work), were denied veteran status and benefits and would not be granted veteran status until 1977. Indeed, this recognition was long overdue, for of the approximately 243,000 merchant mariners that served during the war, over 9,500 died, their casualty rate of 3.9 percent higher than that of any other branch of military service. In fact, the Merchant Marine was a true "weapon" without which the United States could not have won the war, and the Grace Line offers an excellent example. Their peacetime ships, SS *Santa Lucia*, SS *Santa Barbara*, and SS *Santa Clara*, were taken over by the Navy and used as troopships and renamed, in order, USS *Leedstown*, USS *McCawley*, and USS *Susan B. Anthony*. The *Leedstown* was sunk by German dive bombers off Algeria in 1943, while the *McCawley* was sunk at Rendova during the Solomon Islands campaign in 1942 after being damaged by Japanese dive bombers. Finally, USS *Susan B. Anthony* was commanded by Captain Thomas Grey (depicted in the accompanying advertisement), a former Grace Line captain who was accepted into the Navy and continued aboard his old ship, now under a new name. USS *Susan B. Anthony* took part in the invasions of North Africa and Sicily, and later made convoy runs in 1943–44. The ship was lost on June 7, 1944 during the Normandy invasion after striking a mine. The badly damaged ship began listing, but Captain Grey directed the rescue efforts and by his diligence, got all 2,689 people off his ship safely, without loss of life, he being the last to leave his stricken vessel. The saving of his crew and passengers by Captain Grey is thought to be the largest rescue ever of people at sea without any loss of life, and is truly indicative of the service of the Merchant Marine in World War II.

Battle-front U.S.A.

OUR valiant Navy is in action on every ocean, on battle lines stretching around the world. Our proud Merchant Marine, under the leadership of the U. S. Maritime Commission, is carrying the war to the enemy with ever-increasing power.

In Todd Shipyards, on every coast, armies of skilled men are waging another battle . . . fighting against time in the world's greatest shipbuilding program — and beating all records. From day to day, at constantly accelerated pace, hundreds of new merchant vessels and fighting ships of every type will join the mightiest armada in history.

Backed by a hard-hitting maritime tradition, with production at top speed, America swings into the battle line toward Victory!

TODD SHIPYARDS CORPORATION

One Broadway, New York, N. Y.

ins Dry Dock and Repair Co. . . . . . Erie Basin, Brooklyn
en and Lang Dry Dock Co. . . . . . 17th St., Hoboken
tle-Tacoma Shipbuilding Corp. . . . . . Seattle & Tacoma
d Seattle Dry Docks, Inc. . . . . . Seattle
Todd Galveston Dry Docks Inc. . . . . . Galveston
Houston Shipbuilding Corp. . . . . . Houston
Todd-Johnson Dry Docks Inc. . . . . . New Orleans
Todd Mobile Dry Docks Inc. . . . . . Mobile
South Portland Shipbuilding Corp. . . . . . So. Portland, Me.
Todd-Bath Iron Shipbuilding Corp. . . . . . So. Portland, Me.
South Portland Dry Dock & Repair Co. . . . . . So. Portland, Me.
Todd Combustion Equipment, Inc. . . . . . New York

4

Army Air Force Fighters, Bombers, and Other Aircraft

Advertisements for Army Air Force aircraft are among the most numerous and well-produced advertisements of the war. In fact, almost every major aircraft company advertised their wares and the firepower they packed, as did many of the automobile companies who produced them or their components. The official Army letter and numerical designations of each aircraft first identified the type of plane, the "P" standing for "pursuit" aircraft, another term for fighters, the letter "B" designating bomber aircraft, while their numbers were merely technical in nature, largely sequential in terms of when the design was accepted, but not necessarily indicative of when it entered actual service. The Ethyl Corporation (a subsidiary of General Motors and Standard Oil) advertisement shown here highlights all the military aircraft which were powered by their high-octane gasoline.

Fighter Aircraft

Bell P-39 Airacobra

The Bell company was a leader in aviation engineering research and development and built the U.S.'s first military jet, although it saw no wartime use. However, two of their fighters did see combat action, the most important being the P-39 Airacobra. This fighter was of a novel design and was striking in appearance, standing out because of its long nose configuration and the 37-mm cannon mounted there. Unlike most fighters, the engine, an Allison V-12, was mounted behind the pilot's cockpit. Also unusual about the fighter was its tricycle landing gear. Over 9,500 were built during the war, first used by Britain's RAF in 1941, but they found the Airacobra hard to service and ultimately discontinued its use because it was unfit for high-altitude use. However, the Army Air Force did use the P-39 in small numbers for low-level bombing and strafing runs in the Pacific during the fighting in the Solomon Islands. The biggest user by far was the Soviet Union, which received some 5,000 P-39s, over half of all that were produced. Here, where most air-to-air combat took place at lower altitude, the P-39 did well, proving itself to have the needed firepower and durability to help sweep the *Luftwaffe* from Soviet skies. Production of this fighter ended in 1944 when Bell switched to their P-63 fighter production. This interesting ad highlights the nose-firing cannon manufactured by Oldsmobile for the P-39, as well as well as the squadron emblem for the 41st Fighter Squadron that flew the Airacobra, first based in Australia, and then New Guinea in the early years of the war in the Pacific.

Bell P-63 Kingcobra

The design for this fighter, a cousin of the P-39, was submitted ten months before the attack on Pearl Harbor in 1941. While many believe it to be just an improved version of the P-39, it was actually a completely different aircraft, and one more suited to combat than the P-39. This is because the Soviets actually visited the Bell factory in Buffalo, New York, their test pilot offering advice based on their use and experience with the P-39. The Kingcobra was faster by 30 mph than the P-39, clocking in at 410 mph, and had a larger and differently designed wing, as well as a four-bladed propeller, along with other more technical

IN ONE WAY ALL THESE AMERICAN WAR PLANES ARE ALIKE

★ All American fighting planes have one important feature in common: their engines are designed for high-octane gasoline. That's the basic reason why they have more power than similar enemy planes. And because they have more power, they will—plane for plane—outfly and outfight our enemies'.

We alone have *all three* things needed to produce high-octane gasoline—and plenty of it: *one*—vast resources of high quality crude oil; *two*—superior refining processes, developed by America's petroleum industry; *three*—adequate production of anti-knock fluid to improve octane ratings of military gasolines.

The makers of Ethyl brand of anti-knock fluid have geared their plants, laboratories and technical staffs to meet the oil industry's war needs. Until victory is won, our Army, Navy and Allies have first call on Ethyl fluid to make fighting fuels for planes, tanks, armored cars and other mechanized equipment.

AMERICA'S ESOURCES OF HIGH ALITY CRUDE OIL *plus* SUPERIOR REFINING PROCESSES DEVELOPED BY OUR PETROLEUM INDUSTRY *plus* ADEQUATE PRODUCTION OF ANTI-KNOCK FLUID (*containing tetraethyl lead*) = SUPERIOR FIGHTING FUELS

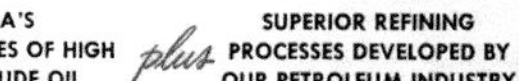
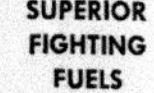

BRAND OF ANTI-KNOCK FLUID — MADE BY THE ETHYL CORPORATION

Flying Buzz-Saw!

OFFICIAL INSIGNIA OF THE 41st FIGHTER SQUADRON U. S. ARMY AIR CORPS

This is only one of the many colorful insignia selected by our Army airmen to identify their squadrons and decorate their planes.

HERE'S TO THE BOYS OF THE "FIGHTING 41st" —*whose courage and ability and fire-power have made this insignia famous. Flying with the same uncanny skill that marks American airmen everywhere, "cutting" Axis formations to ribbons with the fury of their cannon fire . . . these boys are "flying buzz saws" indeed! To them . . . and equally to members of all the other great squadrons of the Army Air Corps . . . Oldsmobile respectfully dedicates this page. More FIRE-POWER for them!*

Note the insignia on the cockpit of this cannon-firing American fighter plane.

FIRE-POWER IS OUR BUSINESS! Putting the "teeth in the buzz saws" is one of our biggest wartime responsibilities at Oldsmobile. The "teeth" are those cannon in the noses of the planes shown in the picture. Tens of thousands have been built at Oldsmobile. And they're still pouring off the lines, to give our flying fighters all the Fire-Power they need. Oldsmobile also supplies another type of airplane cannon — larger, harder-hitting and destined to play a very important role in future aerial warfare. And Oldsmobile produces cannon for tanks and tank destroyers, too, plus s for both Army and Navy . . . Fire-Power action on every front, by land, by sea and by

You too can help back up the boys of the "Fighting 41st." Buy War Bonds regularly.

OLDSMOBILE DIVISION OF GENERAL MOTOR

KEEP 'EM FIRING

Preview of a new Bell Fighter*

* *Described by the Office of War Information as "A new Bell fighter, now in production, with a low drag wing and a two stage, supercharged Allison engine which will make it an efficient plane at any altitude up to 38,000 to 40,000 feet."*

When the Axis powers get their first view of this U. S. Army fighter, just beginning to come off the production lines in our Niagara Frontier plants, they'll see it as a slim, trim, single-engine plane. They'll learn next that it has blinding speed . . . that it can fight effectively high in the sky . . . or blast troops and tanks from tree-top level. Like the Airacobra, "Cannon on Wings," this plane has plenty of firepower. It throws a paralyzing barrage of machine gun bullets and cannon shells.

Manufacturing this new fighter is one part of Bell Aircraft's war job.

Now add four more chapters—(1) building flexible gun mounts for planes and surface ships; (2) designing and building America's first jet propelled plane; (3) developing the new Bell Helicopter; (4) producing bombers in Georgia—and you have the complete story of Bell Aircraft's war effort.

Yes, Bell is concentrating to speed the day of peace. And the lessons we're learning today mean that you can aim *high* when you think about post-war aviation. © Bell Aircraft Corporation.

BUY WAR BONDS AND SPEED VICTORY

MEMBER AIRCRAFT WAR PRODUCTION COUNCIL—EAST COAST, INC

BELL *Aircraft*

PACEMAKER OF AVIATION PROGRESS

Niagara Frontier Division, Buffalo and Niagara Falls, N. Y.—Ordnance Division, Burlington, Vt.—Georgia Division, Marietta, Ga.

design changes. Though it was an improvement over the P-39, by the time it was in production and reached front-line units beginning in October 1943, it was already outdated and rejected by the U.S. Army Air Force in favor of the P-51 Mustang. Despite this, some 3,300 were built, over 2,400 going to the Soviets and at least 300 to the Free French Air Force. Advertisements for this fighter are relatively rare, that by Bell shown here not even mentioning it by name.

Curtiss P-40 Warhawk

This iconic fighter, known for its garishly painted nose featuring a shark's mouth, was designed in 1934 by Curtiss and first designated as the P-36, and overseas versions as the Hawk 75 fighter. Many overseas countries bought the Hawk, especially the French Air Force. After receiving them in early 1939, the Curtiss-built fighter performed well in the Battle of France in May 1940, destroying over 300 German aircraft before France fell. However, the most famous user of this fighter by far was the AVG, the American Volunteer Group (later called the Flying Tigers) flying with the Chinese Air Force of General Chiang Kai-Shek, under the command of General Claire Chennault. The flyers of the AVG, recruited in America, got their start before America entered World War II, but did not begin combat operations until late December 1941, after the attack on Pearl Harbor. They and their P-40 Warhawk fighters first patrolled the skies over the Burma Road, engaging Japanese bombers, its distinctive shark-mouth nose meant to scare the hell out of the enemy. Interestingly, German and British combat aircraft had used the shark-mouth on their combat aircraft prior, but for the P-40 it worked especially well because of its nose design and air-intake configuration. The P-40, now called the Warhawk, was the final variant of the original P-36, noted for the change to the Allison engine in 1937, which had never before been used in aircraft and turned out to be a smashing success. It is for this reason that there were produced numerous advertisements featuring the distinctive shark-mouth P-40, many of them for Allison. With this engine change, the P-40 was obtained by many other Allied nations after 1940, including Britain (who called it the Tomahawk or Kittyhawk), as well as the Soviet Union, Australia, Sweden, and Turkey, and used with great success. Overall, nearly 14,000 P-40 Warhawks of all variants were built and the fighter remains today an iconic symbol of American fighter planes from World War II, this striking ad by General Motors Allison Engine division highlighting its famed nose-art.

Lockheed P-38 Lightning

This big and boldly-designed fighter, built by a company new to the military market, was noted for its twin-booms and its then-new twin Allison engines when its design was submitted in early 1937. What seemed like a very complicated and risky aircraft in its early days turned out to be one of the finest fighters of the war, the first American fighter to have a top-speed in excess of 400 mph. It was soon feared by the Axis powers, said to have been called the "forked-tail devil" by the Germans and "one pilot, two planes" by the Japanese. Because of its distinctive look and legendary performance this fighter was prominently featured in many ads, including those by Lockheed directly, as well as those who supplied components big and small, from Oldsmobile to Champion Spark Plugs. This fighter proved to be one of the most versatile aircraft of the entire war, different variants employed as long-range escorts, on fighter-bomber pathfinder missions, as well as a night fighter and a renowned reconnaissance aircraft which is said to have captured the vast majority of the aerial images taken over Europe during the war. The Lightning achieved success in both the Pacific and European theatres. I have previously referred to this fighter's "Pay-off for Pearl" themed advertisement, illustrative of the strike force of P-38s that dispatched Japan's Admiral Yamamoto, but it was also the fighter flown by America's two top-scoring aces of the war, Major Richard Bong, a Medal of Honor recipient who shot down forty Japanese aircraft while flying the P-38, and Thomas McGuire, also a Medal of Honor recipient, who shot down thirty-eight enemy aircraft before being killed in action over the Philippines in 1945. In Europe, too, the Lightning was a force to be reckoned with early on. It was a pair of P-38s flying from Patterson Field in Reykjavik, Iceland, which scored the first all-American victory against the *Luftwaffe* when they shot down a Focke-Wulf Fw 200 Condor bomber in August 1942. The P-38 was even flown on one mission by American aviation legend Charles Lindbergh in June 1944, he flying with the 475th Satan's Angels Fighter Group in a mission over Jefman Island, shooting up some Japanese barges and small ships. Overall, nearly 10,000 P-38 Lightnings were built during the war, the only American aircraft to be produced during every year of the war and the first fighter to be constructed mainly of stainless steel and aluminum. This ad by Lockheed for the P-38 is interesting for its hopeful, but inaccurate portrayal of a Lightning sporting the roundel emblem of Britain's RAF. The P-38 was never flown by the RAF in combat as they tested three aircraft only early on and deemed them unsuitable, an evaluation that would prove to be very inaccurate.

Straight from the
Tiger's Mouth!
North American Apache (U. S.)
The British call it "The Mustang"
Bell Airacobra
U. S. and British designation
Lockheed P-38 Interceptor (U. S.)
The British call it "The Lightning"
LIQUID-COOLED AIRC

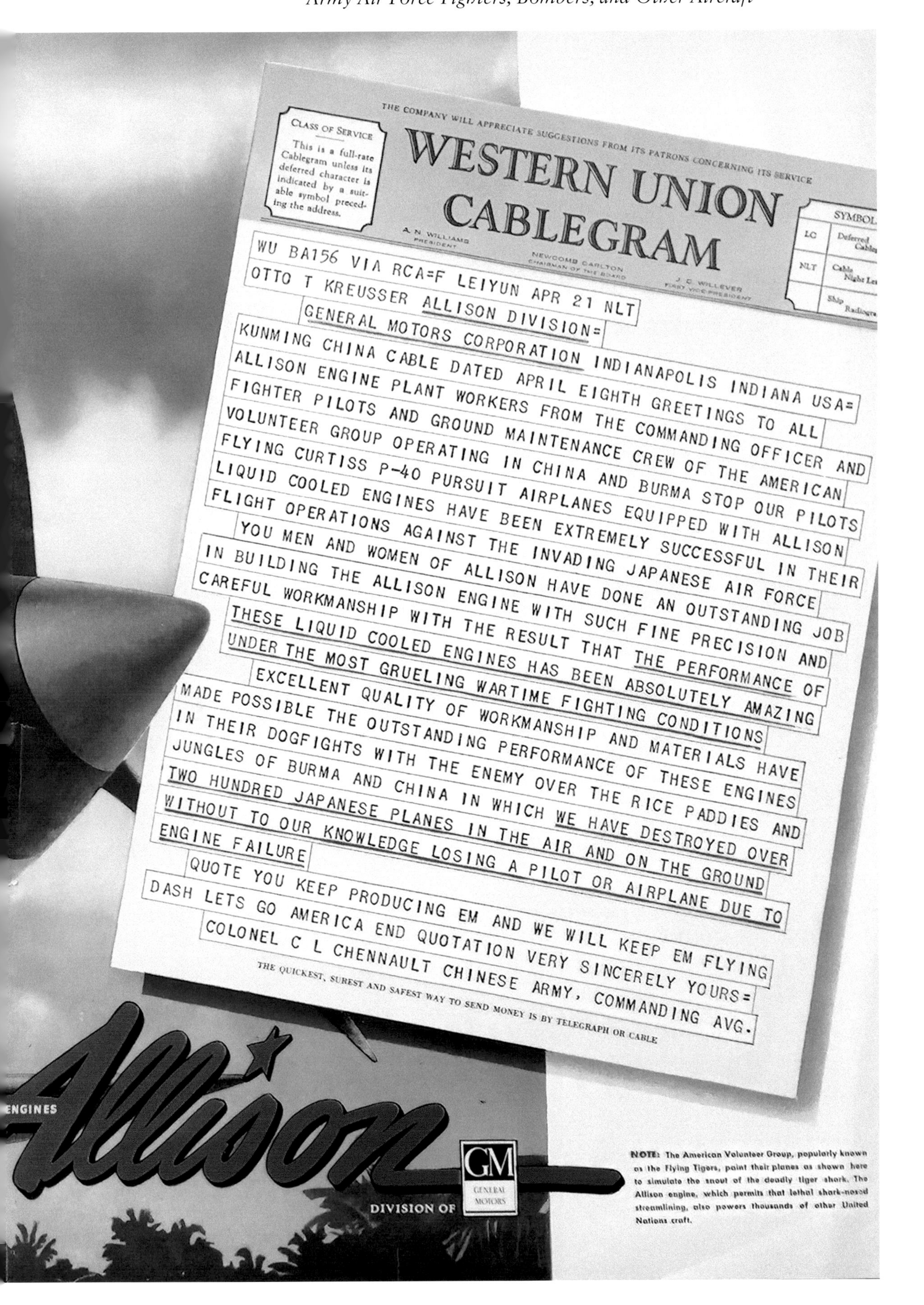

CLASS OF SERVICE
This is a full-rate Cablegram unless its deferred character is indicated by a suitable symbol preceding the address.
THE COMPANY WILL APPRECIATE SUGGESTIONS FROM ITS PATRONS CONCERNING ITS SERVICE
WESTERN UNION CABLEGRAM
A. N. WILLIAMS PRESIDENT
NEWCOMB CARLTON CHAIRMAN OF THE BOARD
J. C. WILLEVER FIRST VICE-PRESIDENT
SYMBOL
LC Deferred
NLT Cable Night
Ship
WU BA156 VIA RCA=F LEIYUN APR 21 NLT
OTTO T KREUSSER ALLISON DIVISION=
GENERAL MOTORS CORPORATION INDIANAPOLIS INDIANA USA=
KUNMING CHINA CABLE DATED APRIL EIGHTH GREETINGS TO ALL
ALLISON ENGINE PLANT WORKERS FROM THE COMMANDING OFFICER AND
FIGHTER PILOTS AND GROUND MAINTENANCE CREW OF THE AMERICAN
VOLUNTEER GROUP OPERATING IN CHINA AND BURMA STOP OUR PILOTS
FLYING CURTISS P-40 PURSUIT AIRPLANES EQUIPPED WITH ALLISON
LIQUID COOLED ENGINES HAVE BEEN EXTREMELY SUCCESSFUL IN THEIR
FLIGHT OPERATIONS AGAINST THE INVADING JAPANESE AIR FORCE
YOU MEN AND WOMEN OF ALLISON HAVE DONE AN OUTSTANDING JOB
IN BUILDING THE ALLISON ENGINE WITH SUCH FINE PRECISION AND
CAREFUL WORKMANSHIP WITH THE RESULT THAT THE PERFORMANCE OF
THESE LIQUID COOLED ENGINES HAS BEEN ABSOLUTELY AMAZING
UNDER THE MOST GRUELING WARTIME FIGHTING CONDITIONS
EXCELLENT QUALITY OF WORKMANSHIP AND MATERIALS HAVE
MADE POSSIBLE THE OUTSTANDING PERFORMANCE OF THESE ENGINES
IN THEIR DOGFIGHTS WITH THE ENEMY OVER THE RICE PADDIES AND
JUNGLES OF BURMA AND CHINA IN WHICH WE HAVE DESTROYED OVER
TWO HUNDRED JAPANESE PLANES IN THE AIR AND ON THE GROUND
WITHOUT TO OUR KNOWLEDGE LOSING A PILOT OR AIRPLANE DUE TO
ENGINE FAILURE
QUOTE YOU KEEP PRODUCING EM AND WE WILL KEEP EM FLYING
DASH LETS GO AMERICA END QUOTATION VERY SINCERELY YOURS=
COLONEL C L CHENNAULT CHINESE ARMY, COMMANDING AVG.
THE QUICKEST, SUREST AND SAFEST WAY TO SEND MONEY IS BY TELEGRAPH OR CABLE
ENGINES
Allison
DIVISION OF
GM
GENERAL MOTORS
NOTE: The American Volunteer Group, popularly known as the Flying Tigers, paint their planes as shown here to simulate the snout of the deadly tiger shark. The Allison engine, which permits that lethal shark-nosed streamlining, also powers thousands of other United Nations craft.

Lightning Strikes

Hard-striking, fast-striking Lightning...a wizard of high-altitude maneuverability ...the Lockheed *Lightning* is a tough-sinewed interceptor, a ship built to reach new sky ceilings—and stay there to take and give plenty of fight.

It is a 'plane made to stop enemy bombers ...dive or long range, high or low altitude... before they get to their objectives.

Built, too, as a fighting guard for our own bombers, it is a 'plane to sweep enemy skies as well as our own, teaming up with other hard-fighting American-built aircraft flying for the United Nations to win air supremacy to win this war.

... for Protection today and Progress tomorrow

LOOK TO *Lockheed* FOR LEADERSHIP

North American P-51 Mustang

Quite simply, the P-51 Mustang was America's finest fighter plane of the war, which says a lot when we consider the other notable American-built fighters including the P-38, the P-47, the Grumman Hellcat, and the F4U Corsair, which also were crucial in winning the war. The development of this fighter was also the most successful fighter program ever, but, ironically, it began under British auspices. RAF representatives approached the North American Aviation company about building the P-40 Warhawk for their use, but that company proposed an entirely new fighter and an agreement was reached. Incredibly, in less than three months in 1940, the Mustang was designed, built, and had its first test flight, with subsequent delivery of the first production fighters in October 1941, and first operational service in January 1942 with the RAF. Unfortunately, the first version of the fighter, distinguished by its tear-drop canopy, bulging nose, and all-aluminum construction, had an Allison engine that performed poorly at high altitude. However, this problem was solved later in 1942 when subsequent Mustangs utilized the high-performing Rolls-Royce Merlin engine, produced under license in America by Packard, and a legend was born. Over 15,500 Mustangs were built during the war, the early model capable of reaching 390 mph, but later and lighter versions capable of 487 mph. This fighter saw its greatest success in escorting American long-range bombers to Germany, providing vital protection during the Allies high-altitude bombing campaign beginning in late 1943. The Mustang, armed with six wing mounted cannons, was also employed on low-level ground attack missions over northern Europe, as well as a reconnaissance aircraft. The Mustang was even employed in downing German V-1 rockets, being one of the few Allied fighters fast enough to intercept them. While the Mustang was largely employed in Europe, it did see Pacific service at the end of the war, escorting B-29s on bombing missions over Japan. Notable users of the P-51 Mustang include Major George Preddy, Jr., who shot down twenty-three enemy aircraft and was the plane's top ace of the war before being killed by friendly fire while in action over Belgium in December 1944, and the Tuskegee Airmen of the 332nd Fighter Group, the first African American fighter group, who began using the fighter in July 1944. This group, which painted the tails of their Mustangs red, taking the nickname "Red Tails," had one of the best records among Mustang fighter groups and not only lost less bombers on their missions than most other groups, but also earned the Distinguished Unit Citation for downing three German Me 262 jets during a mission to Berlin in March 1945. Even after World War II, the Mustang remained the Air Force's primary fighter until it was replaced by jet-powered fighters, and then served in a secondary role until being withdrawn from service in 1957. Even then, Mustangs were used by air forces around the world, last employed by the Dominican Air Force in 1987. Once withdrawn from military service, the Mustang became a popular civilian racing aircraft, and production models for this purpose using original P-51 parts, were manufactured as late as 1972. This ad from North American highlights the acrobatics the nimble Mustang was capable of.

Northrup P-61 Black Widow

Perhaps one of the least-known fighters of the war among the general public, the P-61 was a revolutionary aircraft, which, had it been developed earlier in the war, would have had a greater impact. Most notably, the P-61, nicknamed the Black Widow because it was painted black, was the first American plane ever designed from the ground up as a night fighter, being the first to be equipped with radar as part of its overall design. It was also the most expensive wartime fighter of all, costing some $190,000 apiece to build, as compared to the P-51, a bargain at only $50,000 each. The Black Widow was a big fighter, too, being a twin-boomed aircraft with a center gondola and a 66-foot wingspan, capable of a top speed of up to 440 mph and carrying a crew of three, a pilot, the radar operator, and a gunner. When it first arrived in the European theatre, its use was controversial, many

Mustangs on the Warpath

The forward element is peeling off. The other half of the squadron will fly formation during the attack, providing top cover. That's how P-51 Mustangs take to the warpath over Burma. And what a hunting ground it has been.

Hunting with everything from bazookas to 500 lb. depth charges and 1,000 pound demolition bombs, Mustang pilots have forced the Jap in Burma to move furtively at night and to hide in the jungle during the day.

Like it s famous namesake the P-51 Mustang is tough, fast, hard-hitting and elusive.

North American Aviation *Sets the Pace*

PLANES THAT MAKE HEADLINES...*the P-51 Mustang fighter (A 36 fighter-bomber), B-25 and PBJ Mitchell bomber, the AT-6 and SNJ Texan combat trainer. North American Aviation, Inc. Member, Aircraft War Production Council, Inc.*

considering the lightweight British Mosquito fighter to be faster. The fighter was heavily armed, carrying four fixed 20-mm cannons, highlighted in the ad shown here by Oldsmobile, in its belly and four machineguns in a top turret which was later eliminated. It was also able to carry a bomb load of up to 6,400 lb. The fighter was first proposed in 1940, with the first prototype flown in 1942. Production would not begin until 1944, with fighters first seeing combat in June 1944 in the Pacific, their first kill coming while based on Guadalcanal, and in Europe beginning in July 1944, achieving great success in ground support operations during the Battle of the Bulge in December 1944. After the war ended, aviation technology advancements soon made the P-61, of which about 950 were built, obsolete and it was withdrawn from service in 1954. Because of its late wartime production, few advertisements for the P-61 are to be found.

Republic P-47 Thunderbolt

If ever a World War II fighter deserved more advertising publicity, it had to be this big and successful fighter, nicknamed "The Jug" for its resemblance to a milk bottle. Overshadowed by the P-38 and the P-51, the P-47 Thunderbolt was a vital component of the air war in Europe, with the Eighth Air Force's Thunderbolt-equipped 56th Fighter Group leading the way in air-to-air combat victories, with aces Gabby Gabreski (twenty-eight kills) and Robert Johnson (twenty-seven kills) leading the way. The design of the P-47 was worked out in 1940, with full-scale production beginning in 1942, the first 225 of the P-47s ordered costing $16,275,657, or just over $72,300 apiece. The fighter saw its first combat in April 1943 in Europe and never looked back. The P-47 was a heavy aircraft, weighing in at 9,000 lb. empty, a third greater than the Mustang and just 2,000 lb. less than the twin-engined P-38 Lightning. However, it was fast for its weight, powered by a Pratt & Whitney Double Wasp radial engine and capable of speeds of over 400 mph. Most importantly, it was an extremely rugged fighter and could absorb a great amount of battle-damage and still keep flying. The P-47 was employed in varied roles, mainly as a fighter escort for American bombers, but also in ground attack operations and as a fighter-bomber, the P-47 armed with eight machineguns

and capable of carrying rockets or up to a 2,500-lb. bombload. Though its role as an escort decreased when the P-51 arrived on the scene, the P-47 flew right to the end of the war. Over 15,600 of the P-47 Thunderbolt in all its variants were built at the Republic factory in Farmington, NY, as well as at a new facility in Evansville, Indiana. After the war, the P-47 was phased out of use by 1949, though foreign air forces flew the fighter as late as 1963. The name of this famed fighter is still carried on today in the USAF in the equally famed A-10 Thunderbolt II, a ground-attack jet aircraft that was produced from 1972–1984 by Fairchild-Republic and is still used today. This attractive ad by a rival aircraft manufacturing company highlights the four-bladed props made by Curtiss for the P-47, an excellent example of the cooperative nature of many aircraft-building programs during the war.

Bomber Aircraft

Boeing B-17 Flying Fortress

This iconic bomber is the most famous American bomber of the war, and was the most popular among the Army Air Force personnel who manned them. This bomber got its start in the mid-1930s when the Army was seeking a new and more modern bomber to add to its arsenal. The first Boeing B-17 prototype was flown in 1935, gaining the nickname "Flying Fortress" from a Seattle reporter who coined the term after seeing the many machine guns sticking out from the aircraft. Though a very expensive airplane in its day, the four-engined bomber was first ordered in 1936 and there were some 150 in service by the time of the attack on Pearl Harbor. Production of the B-17 was ramped up quickly and it remained in production into 1945. The most proven version of this bomber was able to attain speeds of 317 mph and had a cruising range of over 1,000 miles. The B-17 was powered by four Studebaker-built, as this ad shows, Wright Cyclone radial engines, the bomber said to be the first combat aircraft to be able to still function if one of its engines failed. In fact, the B-17 could absorb an incredible amount of battle damage and could even fly on just two engines for a short period of time when required. As its nickname implied, the Flying Fortress was well protected, having twin Browning machine guns in the tail, chin, dorsal, and ball turrets, as well as two in the nose, one in the radio compartment, and two in the waist positions. The most exposed gunner positions were the tail gunner and especially the gunner in the ball turret located on the underbelly of the bomber. This was such a cramped space that the ball turret gunner was usually the smallest of the ship's ten-man crew. The standard payload bomb capacity for the B-17 was 6,500lbs, but it could carry up to nearly 13,000 lb. if need be. The early combat record for this bomber was achieved while in service with the RAF in July 1941, and it was an inauspicious start; the Norden bombsight was inaccurate and the earliest version of the B-17 had a blind spot in the tail, which German fighters soon exploited. After limited use, the RAF switched to other bombers and used the few B-17s they had in their Coastal Command forces. However, these experiences led to the design modifications that led to improved models. From the first, American-flown B-17s were involved in combat, with a flight of twelve arriving from California to Hickam Field in Hawaii as the attack on Pearl Harbor was in progress, with two of them lost. The B-17 did serve in the Pacific, but for a short time, a little over a year, before being withdrawn and replaced by the B-24 Liberator, primarily because of its long-range capability. However, it was in Europe where the B-17 made her name, beginning operations there with the Army Air Force's Eighth Air Force beginning in May 1942 with the Allied offensive bombing campaign, which involved around the clock raids deep into Germany, the Americans taking the dangerous day-time raids, while the RAF contributed massive night-time raids. It was during this extended and grueling campaign in which famed aircraft like the *Memphis Belle* (her exploits documented in book and film) flew twenty-five combat missions over France and Germany between November 1942 and May 1943 before returning to the U.S. to be part of a war-bond tour, made their mark. While the bomber remained in service through the end of the war, by that time its shorter range and slower speed in comparison to other bombers meant that its time was coming to an end. Nearly 13,000 B-17s in all rolled off the production line, with many of their engines built by automobile companies like Studebaker, but after the war they were quickly phased out and relegated to a transport and air-sea rescue role before their final phaseout in the 1950s. As with other wartime aircraft, surplus B-17s were acquired by the air forces of other nations and used by them for years, the last active user being the Brazilian Air Force, which retired its B-17s in 1968. While there is a great debate to this day about which bomber, the B-17 or the B-24, was the better one, there is no doubt that in terms of publicity and popularity, the B-17 Flying Fortress was the victor in the hearts and minds of the American public.

Boeing B-29 Superfortress

This bomber was, by far, the most technical airplane ever built for the military up to that time, and it was massive in size, as its name implies. Powered by four Wright Duplex Cyclone radial engines, the B-29 could reach a speed of 357 mph and operate at 32,000 feet, carrying a bomb load of up to 20,000 lb. Its wingspan was 141 feet as compared to the B-17's 104 feet, and it was 99 feet long, some 25 feet longer than the B-17. It was the first U.S. bomber to be built with computerized controls and a pressurized cabin, which enabled her to operate at the greater height, and had a range of just over 3,200 miles, nearly triple that of the B-17. Indeed, the B-29 was a Superfortress in every way, costing about $640,000 per plane, its entire development program said to cost nearly double that of the Manhattan Project with which the bomber would be intimately connected. The B-29, of which nearly 4,000 were built, was at first planned to be deployed in Germany, and then switched to the Pacific, but this policy changed and the bomber was solely used in the Pacific during the war. They began arriving at air bases in China and India in the spring of 1944, and flew their first mission in June 1944 when at least seventy-seven (and possibly as many as 114) departed from a base in India to bomb railroad facilities, a bridge, and a power-plant in Bangkok, Thailand. Following that test mission, later in the month, the first B-29 bombing mission to Japan would follow, thereby setting the tone of its missions for the remainder of the war. Once the Mariana Islands were captured, B-29 bases were moved there and missions to Japan were flown from Tinian, Saipan, and Guam beginning in October 1944. In November 1944, 111 B-29 Superforts hit the Japanese capital of Tokyo, the first strike on that city since the Doolittle Raid in April 1942. From there on out, the B-29s rained fire and destruction down on the Japanese homeland, destroying Japanese cities and ruining its wartime economy. The B-29 Superfortress, for many, is best known for being the aircraft that dropped the first ever atomic bombs, first on Hiroshima on August 6, 1945 when the bomber *Enola Gay*, flown by Lt. Col. Paul Tibbetts, dropped the Little Boy bomb. The second atomic bomb, called Fat Man, was dropped by the B-29 named *Bock's Car* on Nagasaki on August 9. Both of these B-29s are in museums today, the *Enola Gay* at one of the Smithsonian's museums in Washington, D.C., and the other at the National Museum of the U.S. Air Force in Dayton, Ohio. As a result of the B-29's offensive, the Japanese government finally sued for peace on August 15. While the dropping of the atomic bomb may be forever debated, military leaders at the time viewed it as the best answer to a problem that had no good solution, knowing that the alternative, an amphibious assault on Japan, would result in as many as 1 million military casualties. Following the end of the war, the B-29 remained in the arsenal of the new independent USAF, and was used for bombing missions during the Korean War until the advent of Soviet jet fighter aircraft made it vulnerable. It continued in secondary roles until being retired from service in the mid-1960s. This ad is unusual for depicting an Asian boy (probably Chinese as B-29s operated out of bases in and helped liberate that country) flashing the V for Victory sign when few other ads depict any non-whites.

Consolidated B-24 Liberator

This notable bomber has, perhaps, one of the most confusing legacies of the war, a versatile aircraft that is misunderstood by many to this day and one that will forever be overshadowed by the more glamorous B-17 Flying Fortress. In fact, aviation historian Bill Gunston calls the B-24 Liberator "one of the most important in the history of aviation." This bomber, of which over 19,000 were built, more than any other military aircraft in history, came into existence in an ironic manner. In 1938, the Army asked the Consolidated Vultee Aircraft Company of San Diego to build the B-17 under license, but the company decided to build a bomber on their own instead. They submitted their design in 1939, the Army seeking a bomber that was faster, and could fly higher and farther than the B-17. What Consolidated came up with was a good step in that direction, and a revolutionary one to boot. The whole aircraft was unusual looking, its most notable feature being its so-called Davis wing, which was more slender than the typical wing on such a large airplane of the day and being mounted high on the fuselage. This new wing design was key in enabling the Liberator to fly faster and farther due to its high efficiency. Also distinctive was the tail configuration, featuring large, twin oval-shaped stabilizers rather than the typical single fin carried by most aircraft. The B-24 was also the first U.S. bomber to have tricycle-style landing gear, which often proved to be problematic when the bomber operated from more primitive airstrips. Nicknamed the "flying boxcar" for the look of its big and wide fuselage, the Liberator, unlike the B-17, was never noted for its beauty. However, a bomber is not judged on its look, but rather by its performance, and by that measure the B-24 was a smashing success, as the numbers of them built will testify to. Powered by four Pratt & Whitney

LET'S FINISH THE JOB
Buy Extra War Bonds

DEAN CORNWELL

The Army-Navy "E" flies above seven Fisher Body plants for excellence in aircraft production and from two others for tank production, while the Navy "E," with five stars, is flown by still another Fisher Body plant for its naval ordnance work.

STRICTLY SUPER

IT'S a great day for our side whenever our flyers sweep out over the target in those fleets of B-29 Superfortresses.

Of course, Fisher Body does not make the complete Superfortress. But it does make huge dorsal fins, horizontal stabilizers, rudders, elevators and ailerons. Yes, and flaps, wing tips, outboard wings and turret parts, too.

More than that, Fisher Body makes engine nacelles — using more than 18,000 jigs and tools to turn out the 3,000 parts that are required for each nacelle.

Fisher Body is proud of its part in building this great Boeing-designed ship. All the skills and techniques inherent in the Fisher Body organization are concentrated on giving superworkmanship to the Superfortress. Yet it is but one of many war jobs including big guns, delicate aircraft instruments, tanks, and assemblies for other bombers.

And you may be certain that as long as war equipment is needed, the fine craftsmanship symbolized by the "Body by Fisher" emblem will keep right on backing up the courageous crews who pilot these great superplanes.

Every Sunday Afternoon
GENERAL MOTORS SYMPHONY OF THE AIR
NBC Network

DIVISION OF GENERAL MOTORS

Twin Wasp radial engines (many built by Buick), the Liberator, said to have been given this name by Winston Churchill, had a top speed of 290 mph, had a range of 2,200 miles (twice that of the B-17), and could fly as high as 28,000 feet. Its bomb capacity was 8,000 lb., and for protection had ten Browning machine guns, two each in the tail, nose, dorsal, and ball turrets, as well as two in the waist positions. Like the B-17, the bomber operated with a crew of ten men. Though the B-24 outperformed the B-17 in many aspects, it was also very difficult to fly and somewhat less stable than the B-17. For this reason, the B-24 was less popular in general with American bomber crews. The first Liberators to enter service came off the production line in 1940, first intended for the French Air Force, but once that country fell to the Germans they were assigned to the RAF. However, the Liberator was not first used as a bomber, but as a transport aircraft flying between Canada and Scotland, as well as being assigned to RAF Coastal Command for anti-submarine work. The RAF subsequently would use the Liberator in the Middle East, but not in the bombing campaign in Europe. The bomber first saw combat with U.S. Army forces in the Pacific in June 1942, and from that time forth it would be the dominant bomber in that theatre until the advent of the B-29. The B-24 was also a major component of the European bombing campaign, first seeing action while flying from airfields in Egypt in June 1942 to bomb the oil refineries around Ploesti, Romania. Their combat service was extended in late 1942 when B-24 bomb groups began flying from airfields in Italy. The most famed raid in the bomber's history was that on Ploesti, again, in August 1943, when a force of 177 B-24s flew long-distance from an airfield in Benghazi, Libya, without fighter escort in an effort to knock Ploesti's oil refineries out of the war for good. Code-named Operation Tidal Wave, the mission was a difficult one that met with only small success, disabling their targets for only a short time, but it was also one that was filled with bravery and demonstrated the toughness of the Liberator. Five pilots on this mission, three of whom were killed in action, earned the Medal of Honor, and fifty-four of the bombers were lost. It was one of the most epic air-battles of the entire war, one in which a number of badly damaged or crippled Liberators made it back to either their home base or a neutral airfield after being chopped up by flak and German fighters. To this last point, it has often been stated that, in comparison to the B-17, the B-24 was more of a death-trap, somehow more easily shot down or less likely to survive battle-damage. However, the final statistics fail to bear this out, as casualty rates of those units which flew Liberators were slightly lower than that of the B-17. In reality, the B-24, like the B-17, should be celebrated for its contribution to winning the war, it being used in a wide variety of roles, as a bomber, as an assembly ship, a transport, anti-submarine work, tanker, and reconnaissance aircraft, more so than any other airplane of the war.

Douglas A-20 Havoc/Boston

This hard-hitting aircraft is probably one of the least remembered of the fighter planes of the war, overshadowed by fighters like the P-38. However, the fact remains that the Havoc was an excellent performer and played an important role in both Europe and the Pacific, despite the fact that only about 7,400 were built between 1939 and 1944. When in 1937 the Army was looking for an attack aircraft, Douglas entered the competition to gain a contract, with their prototype making its first flight in 1938. While the U.S. Army showed little interest, the French did, ordering the first production fighters after specified modifications were made, which were delivered beginning in late 1940. The Havoc, as it was called by the U.S. Army, first flew in combat with the French Air Force during the German Blitzkrieg in May 1940. Once France fell, some of these fighters escaped to North Africa, while others were taken over by the Vichy government. Those remaining fighters that had not yet been delivered by Douglas were subsequently sent to Britain and used by the RAF. Designated as the Boston by the British, this fighter was employed by them as a night fighter and an intruder aircraft, and later as a medium bomber. Capable of reaching a speed of about 350 mph, this twin-engined fighter bomber was capable of packing a punch and performed well in the North African campaign. By now, the U.S. Army also had an interest in the improved version of the Havoc, and it subsequently saw its first combat action for them in the Pacific at New Guinea in August 1942. The A-20s that were flown by bomb groups in the Pacific used the Havoc in low-level missions and added extra machine guns in the nose to make it even more deadly. Despite these uses, over half of the A-20s were sent via Lend-Lease to the Soviet Union and they subsequently used more of them than the U.S., employing them in a similar role as a low-level fighter and bomber. Once the war was over, the A-20 was soon retired by the USAF in 1949. The United-Carr company originally got its start in the 1920s making automobile top and side-curtain fasteners.

"GET UP THERE AND SLUG

It takes all kinds of planes to make an air force.

Sleek fighters. Swift interceptors. High-level bombers bristling with defensive armament.

And perhaps you'd like to know where, in this line-up, the B-24 Liberator fits in.

Well, it's swift. Not so long ago it made the headlines for the world's record Atlantic crossing – six hours, twenty minutes flying time.

Again, this plane's job is to carry a world-famed figure on missions of global strategy.

Sometimes you've heard about it in North Africa, or over the Channel, or peppering the long, battered boot that was Rome's glory.

"Liberator" to you, it's rapidly becoming "Nemesis" to the Axis—because this big, swift, four-engined ship with its broad belly full of bombs is ideal when the command is "Get up there—and slug!"

BUICK DIVISION OF GENERAL

BETTER
BUY
BONDS
"
Ve're proud of the Liberator's record ecause we build its engines.
he four mighty Pratt & Whitney en- ines with which it starts in life come by he many-hundreds monthly from busy uick plants.
Ve think a lot, as we build those en- ines, about the men who will ride eside them.
hey get in the licks wherever there's job to do. Just "git there fustest with the mostest" bombs.
They count a lot on their engines – both to get them over the target before they are spotted and to get away from intercepting fighters.
So they count on us. And whatever it takes – *we're not going to let them down!*
VICTORY
is our
Business
GM
war goods
WHEN BETTER AUTOMOBILES ARE BUILT
BUICK WILL BUILD THEM
ARMY
E
NAVY
MOTORS
The Army-Navy "E" proudly flies over Buick plants in both Flint, Mich., and Melrose Park, Ill., having been awarded to Buick people for outstanding performance in the production of war goods.

ON THE Douglas A-20 HAVOC

Airloc

COWL FASTENERS ARE STANDARD EQUIPMENT

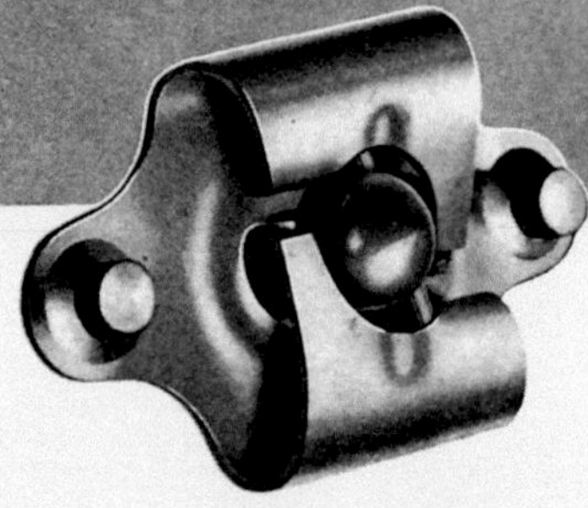

UNITED-CARR FASTENER CORPORATION CAMBRIDGE 42, MASS.

DECEMBER 1 1944

205

Douglas A-26 Invader

This twin-engined attack bomber was the successor to the Douglas A-20, its entire development and building history accomplished during World War II. Though it came along late in the war and was better known for its subsequent service in the Korean and Vietnam Wars, the Invader was an important warplane that, like its predecessor, played a dual role. The first prototype flew in 1942 and production of the powerful plane, armed with ten machine guns, some variants having up to eight in the nose, and capable of carrying an internal bomb load of 4,000 lb., later increased to 8,000 lb. with the addition of external wing mounts. Powered with two Pratt & Whitney radial engines, the Invader could reach speeds up to 355 mph. A total of about 2,500 Invaders were built overall, the attack bomber being used in both the Pacific and European theatres. As with many new fighting aircraft, the first Invaders to see action, arriving there in June 1944, were rejected as unfit for use because the view from the cockpit was obscured by the engines, making them poorly suited for low-level missions. Once the A-26 was redesigned with a glass nose to improve visibility, it returned to action in the Pacific in early 1945, but few missions were flown. In Europe, Douglas hoped to redeem the A-26, flying their first missions in September 1944 with the 416th Bomb Group. In this theatre, the A-26 was a popular bomber and it ended up flying over 11,000 missions up to the end of the war, serving as a low-level bomber and ground attack fighter, as well as a night fighter and fast reconnaissance plane. After the end of the war, at a time when many World War II aircraft were fast rendered obsolete, the A-26 Invader, now called the B-26, held its own, serving as bomber and ground attack fighter in the Korean War, while during the Vietnam War, it was upgraded for use in counter-insurgency missions in emergency fashion after the fighter suffered several instances of catastrophic structural failure. The last Invader was retired from service in 1972. The accompanying ad for Beech Aircraft documents how small civilian aircraft manufacturers put their expertise to work on a larger scale during the war years.

Lockheed Hudson

This twin-engined reconnaissance bomber/transport was built by Lockheed in response to the British need for just such an aircraft at a time when British manufacturers were struggling to produce enough regular fighters and bombers for the RAF. The Lockheed design was an easy one, based on their peacetime Super Electra airliner that was modified for military use, with a prototype developed in late 1938, and the first aircraft of over 250 initially ordered delivered in early 1939. Though not a fast airplane, the Hudson was very maneuverable and had a range of nearly 2,000 miles, able to carry a 750-lb. bomb load. The Hudson was armed with seven machine guns overall, including two in the distinctive rear dorsal turret, and was capable of performing many tasks, employed as a bomber, reconnaissance aircraft, as well as by RAF Coastal Command in anti-submarine duties. About 3,000 were built overall, most going to the RAF, and about 500 for the USAAF. Among its many distinguished contributions to the war, several stand out above all others; it was an RAF Hudson that downed the first enemy aircraft while based on British soil during World War II, doing so in October 1939, while a Hudson of the Royal Australian Air Force (RAAF) made the first Allied attack against the Japanese in the Pacific war when it bombed and sank a Japanese troop transport during their invasion of Malaya, just over an hour before the attack on Pearl Harbor in December 1941. In the Battle of Dunkirk in May 1940, Hudsons were employed as fighters, helping to provide cover and battle the Luftwaffe during the evacuation of Allied troops. Perhaps its greatest, and most bizarre, feat came in August 1941, when an RAF Hudson from 269 Squadron, based in Iceland, bombed and damaged *U-570*. The submarine surfaced, and with the boat unable to dive and her commander afraid the U-boat might be strafed or bombed again, waved a white flag to surrender, the Hudson remaining above the submarine until Royal Navy ships arrived on the scene to secure the U-boat, and subsequently towed her to port as a prize, gaining valuable intelligence in the process. It is the only known case of an aircraft capturing an enemy submarine intact. In addition to being flown by the British, Aussies, and the Americans, the Hudson was also flown in combat by the Royal New Zealand Air Force (RNZAF) with similar successful results.

Martin B-26 Marauder

Built by the pioneering firm of Glenn L. Martin, which built early bombers for the U.S. Army in support of the new doctrines demonstrated by General Billy Mitchell in the 1920s, this twin-engined medium bomber, manned by a crew of seven, was used extensively in the European theatre, and to a small degree in the Pacific. Despite the fact that the B-26 was obsolete by the war's end, with her numerical designation given over to the

The Douglas A-26 Invaders are helping to carry the fight to the enemy. ¶ Beechcrafters are building complete wing assemblies, including engine nacelles and flaps, for the deadly A-26; in addition to the production of Beechcrafts for our Armed Services and those of our Allies. ¶ Beechcrafters are carrying a greater War Production load than ever before, but are proud to make this worthwhile extra contribution to early Victory. ¶ They ask the indulgence of prospective peacetime Beechcraft customers for their complete preoccupation with production for Victory. ¶ To the thousands of Beechcrafters in the Armed Services, and to all other service men and women everywhere, they send greetings and repledge themselves to do everything and anything within their power to bring Victory at the earliest possible moment.

Douglas A-26 Invader (see above), this bomber, after many tribulations, achieved the lowest loss rate of any U.S. bomber during the war. It was fast, clocking in at a top speed of over 300 mph, and carried a bomb load of up to 5,200 lb., later reduced to 4,000 lb., and was armed with up to twelve machine guns in some variants. The B-26 was designed beginning in 1939, with the first production bombers delivered in early 1941. The bomber had initial problems with the wings and, after a number of fatal accidents, the problems were eventually corrected. Despite this fix, the B-26 remained a hard aircraft to fly and it was generally unpopular to fly among Army pilots. To combat this negative image, the Martin company commissioned many favorable articles about the bomber, as well as an extensive advertising campaign, and it is for this reason that B-26 ads are quite easy to find in period magazines. The Marauder first saw action in the South Pacific in April 1942, employed in attacking the major Japanese base at Rabaul, while months later, units were based on New Caledonia, participating in the Solomon Islands campaign. By 1943, the B-26 was beginning to be replaced by the B-25, but continued to be used in the Pacific into 1944. The B-26 saw its first use against the Germans in the North African campaign, and subsequently the Italian campaign, but suffered heavy losses in comparison to the B-25. The B-26 flew its first mission over Europe in May 1943, the low-level operations a disaster, in one case an entire flight of eleven B-26s lost to German fighters and antiaircraft fire during a mission over Holland. After this time, the B-26 was employed in medium-altitude operations with the 9th Air Force, and this is where, finally, the B-26 found her niche, being the most accurate bomber in the final stages of the war. The B-26 was also flown by the South African Air Force, employed in operations over the Aegean Sea, while the Free French Air Force also flew three squadrons of Marauders during Operation Dragoon, the Allied invasion of southern France, in August 1944. Among the companies that manufactured this bomber on their assembly lines was the DeSoto Division of Chrysler.

North American B-25 Mitchell

This medium bomber was built in greater numbers, nearly 10,000 in all, than any other twin-engined combat aircraft, and is considered by many to be the finest medium bomber of the war. The bomber was first designed in 1939, with development taking several years until B-25s began rolling off the assembly line in 1941. B-25 units became operational in 1942, the Mitchell making a big name for itself with the famed Doolittle Raid in April 1942. In this, the first attack launched on the Japanese homeland, sixteen B-25s, led by Col. Jimmy Doolittle, flew off the deck of the carrier USS *Hornet* to make their daring raid on Tokyo. Not only did the raid stun the Japanese people, but it raised morale at home in the wake of the Pearl Harbor attack, and it was the first time such a large aircraft had ever taken off from the deck of a carrier. The raid was later memorialized in the famed 1943 book, and subsequent movie, *30 Seconds Over Tokyo*, written by B-25 pilot Captain Ted Lawson. It also led to the B-25 being featured in many wartime advertisements, more so than most other combat aircraft. Early versions of the B-25 were lightly armed with but four machine guns, but later variants carried a nose-mounted 75-mm gun and fourteen machine guns, while it was capable of delivering a bomb payload of 4,000 lb. Most B-25s were used in the Pacific, serving as ground attack bombers, as well as a deadly anti-shipping aircraft, in addition to its regular bombing duties. As to its use in the skies over Europe, it was first flown by the RAF beginning in early 1943 and employed on bombing missions, and later by the many squadrons that employed the Mitchell in the U.S. Army's Ninth and Twelfth Air Forces flying out of Italy. Among the men flying in this versatile aircraft was a young bombardier named Joseph Heller, serving in the 488th Bombardment Squadron and flying some sixty missions before returning to civilian life. He would later use this military wartime experience as the backdrop for his famed novel *Catch-22*. Overall, the B-25 Mitchell was regarded as an easy aircraft to fly and one that could complete its mission, absorb battle-damage, and get its crews home safely. After the war, a small number of B-25s remained in Air Force use, the last one retired in 1960.

Other Aircraft

CURTISS C-46 COMMANDO

This troop and cargo carrier first arrived on the scene as a civilian airliner in 1936, but in 1940, it was redesigned for military use, primarily by the Army, but also for the Navy. Overall, about 3,300 of these twin-engined aircraft were built, capable of carrying about forty troops and 12,000 lb. of cargo. It is most distinguished as being the plane used to carry supplies over "The Hump," the route between India and China over the Himalayan Mountains that helped keep the Chinese war effort resupplied. However, by 1944, the C-46 was also employed in Europe, most notably during the Allies crossing of the Rhine River. For many years after the war, well into the 1980s, the Commando was in use as a cargo carrier throughout the world, often flying in primitive conditions.

DOUGLAS C-47 SKYTRAIN/DAKOTA

This twin-engined transport was a military version of the famed Douglas DC-3 civilian airliner and was first adapted for military use beginning in December 1941. It is, without a doubt, the most iconic transport aircraft of the war and was used very successfully in both the China–Burma theatre, as well as in Europe. The transport, of which over 10,000 were built, was widely used by many nations. In the U.S. Army it was called the Skytrain, but in RAF and Commonwealth service it was known as the Dakota. The transport was used in a wide number of roles and had many variants, depending on its use. It gained fame flying The Hump, the air route between India and China, as well as in the Pacific, where naval versions transported troops into Guadalcanal and New Guinea. In Europe, the C-47 gained great fame towing gliders loaded with troops during airborne landings, as well as transporting paratroopers, including men of the famed 82nd and 101st Airborne divisions during the Normandy invasion in June 1944. Over 1,000 C-47s were used during this operation, many pilots doing brave service getting troops to their destination in the face of overwhelming enemy fire. The C-47 was also used to resupply beleaguered American troops during the Battle of Bastogne. In short, this transport could do it all, and even after World War II, it was an important aircraft,

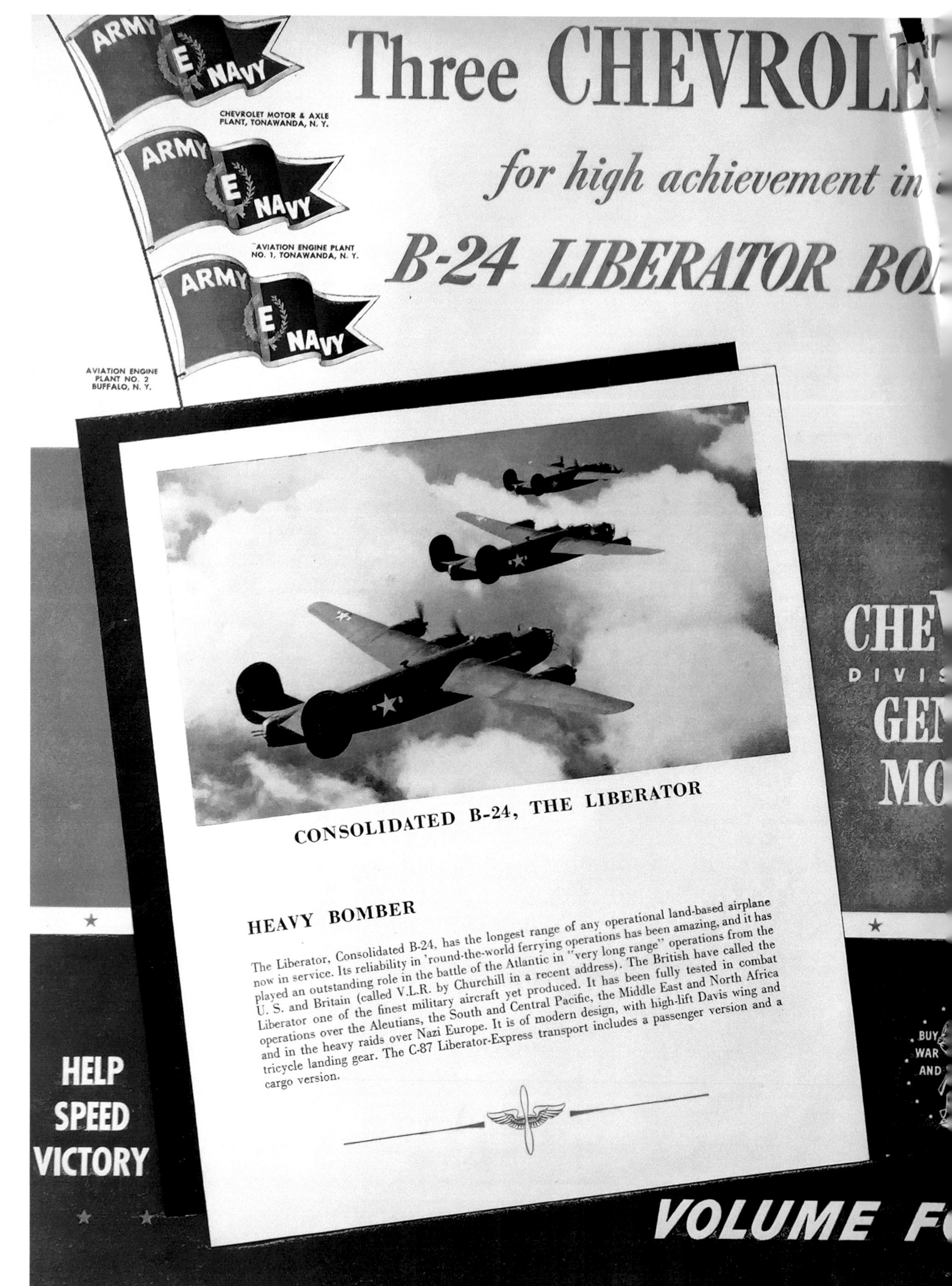
ARMY E NAVY
CHEVROLET MOTOR & AXLE PLANT, TONAWANDA, N. Y.
ARMY E NAVY
AVIATION ENGINE PLANT NO. 1, TONAWANDA, N. Y.
ARMY E NAVY
AVIATION ENGINE PLANT NO. 2 BUFFALO, N. Y.
Three CHEVROLE
for high achievement in
B-24 LIBERATOR BO
CONSOLIDATED B-24, THE LIBERATOR
HEAVY BOMBER
The Liberator, Consolidated B-24, has the longest range of any operational land-based airplane now in service. Its reliability in 'round-the-world ferrying operations has been amazing, and it has played an outstanding role in the battle of the Atlantic in "very long range" operations from the U. S. and Britain (called V.L.R. by Churchill in a recent address). The British have called the Liberator one of the finest military aircraft yet produced. It has been fully tested in combat operations over the Aleutians, the South and Central Pacific, the Middle East and North Africa and in the heavy raids over Nazi Europe. It is of modern design, with high-lift Davis wing and tricycle landing gear. The C-87 Liberator-Express transport includes a passenger version and a cargo version.
CHE
DIVIS
GE
MO
BUY WAR AND
HELP SPEED VICTORY
VOLUME F

Plants Fly Army-Navy "E" Flags

nanufacture of Pratt & Whitney Engines for

ERS and C-47 and C-53 CARGO PLANES

OLET
N OF
RAL
RS

DOUGLAS C-47, THE SKYTRAIN

CARGO TRANSPORT

The Skytrain and Skytrooper (Douglas C-47 and C-53) are military versions of the silver DC-3 airliner, so familiar over American airports, and even before the present conflict in use by nearly a score of foreign countries throughout the world. The Skytrain has a reinforced floor bottom and large loading doors for cargo, and the Skytrooper is fitted with jump seats, being used for military passengers, parachutists or airborne infantry. Both types are to some degree interchangeable, however, and both can quickly be adapted for emergency use for evacuating the wounded, in addition to which there is a special "air ambulance" version normally used for this purpose. C-47's have been carrying the ball on vital air supply routes, and were used heavily in flying thousands of troops, with all their equipment, ammunition, food and supplies, over the Owen Stanley Mountains in the campaign which cleared the enemy out of eastern New Guinea. From the start of the North Africa campaign, when 47 of these planes flew several hundred fully equipped paratroopers from England to the landing point in Africa, a trip of nearly 1500 miles, and straight through to the final victory, the Skytrains maintained a constant shuttle service for both the Troop Carrier unit and the Air Service unit.

NDS
AMPS

BUY
WAR
BONDS

R VICTORY

being used in the Berlin Airlift, while a heavily armed version saw service in Vietnam doing counter-insurgency work. To this day, a few C-47s still remain operational, used by private companies. As this ad shows, Chevrolet contributed to the building of the C-47 by making her Pratt & Whitney engines.

Douglas C-54 Skymaster

Like the C-47 Skytrain, the Douglas C-54 was a derivative of a civilian airliner, their bigger DC-4. This airliner did not meet with success in the U.S., but in 1938, a military version was proposed. In 1941, the Army took over production of this modified airliner turned transport, with the first aircraft coming off the production line in 1942. This bigger transport, distinguished by its shiny metal finish, was powered by four Pratt & Whitney engines, was an excellent performer, though always overshadowed by the C-47, and about 1,250 in all were built. It too was used to carry troops and pull gliders, and one version was specially built with a wheelchair lift to transport President Roosevelt. After the war, the C-54 was the mainstay transport during the Berlin Airlift and was used by the Air Force as late as 1972 and the Navy in 1974. The aircraft was also used as a civilian airliner around the world for many years, as late as 2012 by some charter companies.

North American T-6 Texan

Perhaps the most famous advanced training aircraft in history, this plane was first produced as a civilian aircraft in 1935, but would come to be used by the USAAF, the RAF, and many other air forces around the world as their main trainer during World War II. Indeed, over 15,000 were built from 1938–45, and though they were not designed for combat use (though they were used in that role by the Syrian Air Force in the Arab–Israeli War in 1948), they were flown by countless pilots who went on to fly bomber, fighter, and transport aircraft during the war. The T-6, called the Harvard by RAF and Commonwealth air forces, was used as a trainer by countries around the world, as this ad highlights, and remained popular after the war, being used by the South African Air Force as late as 1995. For many years, and to this day, it has been a popular feature at air shows around the world.

Waco CG-4A Haig Assault Glider

This engine-less aircraft was the main glider used by the U.S. Army during the war and was first built in 1942. It was constructed of fabric covered wood and metal, being 48 feet long, able to carry thirteen to fifteen fully-equipped troops or about 3,700 lb. of cargo (including a jeep or small artillery piece), crewed by a pilot and co-pilot. The Haig was typically towed to its destination by a C-47 or other transport, pulled on a towline which was 350 feet long. The glider could withstand speeds up to 125 mph, and when untethered, travelled somewhere between 40 and 65 mph. Piloting these assault gliders was a dangerous job; they offered no armored protection from enemy fighters, and collisions or a rough landing, striking even a small tree, could result in the front of the glider being totally stove in, killing her crew. This same held true for any cargo that came loose during a landing, which could potentially crush to death the troops being carried or the pilots forward. About 13,000 were built during the war by sixteen different companies, including Cessna, Ford Motor Co., the Ward Furniture Company, and Gibson Refrigerator. They were first used during the Allied invasion of Sicily in July 1943, and several thousand were used during the D-Day invasion of Normandy. After the war, all the gliders were declared surplus and sold off, many reclaimed for their wood, but many, with their nose and tail cut off, were converted to campers and hunting cabins. The Celanese Celluloid Company advertisement highlights the light-weight plastic components it supplied in the making of this glider.

Sikorsky R-4 Helicopter

Seldom do we think of the helicopter as a World War II weapon, it having a greater association with the Korean and Vietnam Wars. However, this pioneer aircraft did indeed see limited use at the end of the war. This two-seat helicopter, designed by Russian immigrant Igor Sikorsky, first flew in a demonstration in 1940, and, after being accepted by the Army, saw its first service flight in 1942. From 1942–44, 131 were built (forty-five going to the RAF, three to the Coast Guard), the Army accepting their first prototypes in 1943. The R-4 saw its first operational use in January 1944 after an explosion sank the destroyer USS *Turner* off New York, when Coast Guard Lt. Cdr. Frank Erikson transported two cases of plasma from New York to a hospital in Sandy Hook, used to save the destroyer's injured crewmen. It was the first use ever of a helicopter in a life-saving role. Later, in April 1944, an RH-4 of the 1st Air Commando Group rescued four men from a downed transport in the China–Burma–India theatre. The RH-4 was also used in the Pacific to transport the wounded, as well as to ferry badly needed aircraft parts from one location to another. This early ad for Sikorsky highlights the fact that their wartime production was achieved through Nash-Kelvinator company.

Douglas Builds All Three

When United Nations air strategy called for concentration on eavy bombers and transports, only Douglas was chosen to produce ll three current 4-engine types: Douglas' own C-54 Skymaster ombat Transport (bottom), the B-24 Liberator Bomber and the lying Fortress. Douglas production of "big brutes" has been n schedule or ahead of schedule, in addition to fabulous output f more other types of aircraft than any other manufacturer.

DOUGLAS

Douglas Aircraft Co., Santa Monica, Calif.
LONG BEACH, EL SEGUNDO, and DAGGETT, CALIF.
TULSA, OKLAHOMA OKLAHOMA CITY CHICAGO

Barrage Balloons

This airborne weapon, while "not of primary importance" by the Army Air Force's own admission and a hold-over technology from World War I, was nonetheless an interesting aspect of World War II operations. There were two types of these balloons, those designed to operate at very low altitude, and those which operated at a high altitude, they ranging anywhere from about 30 to 75 feet long. Their mode of operation was quite simple, and the same as they were deployed in World War I. They were flown over important installations such as ports and beachheads as a deterrent to enemy bombers, they taking up airspace (and some equipped with close-contact explosives) to prevent low-level bombing runs, forcing the bombers to operate at a higher level, hopefully with greater inaccuracy. The Army developed a barrage balloon program before the war and began to form barrage balloon battalions. After the attack on Pearl Harbor in December 1941, barrage balloons would be deployed over such cities as Seattle and San Francisco on the west coast to protect their wartime industries from possible Japanese air raids. They would also be deployed in the northeast over cities like New York to prevent possible German attacks. However, by the end of 1942, with no attacks coming from the air and more modern anti-aircraft defenses in place, the Army removed the balloons. However, though the technology was a dying one, they would be deployed to the Mediterranean theatre, where barrage balloons helped protect such ports as Oran during the North African campaign from German dive-bombers in 1943, and they were also used to protect the Italian port of Naples in early 1944. This was the greatest extent of their combat use, though the image of barrage balloons in the sky during the D-Day invasion of Normandy is an iconic one. It was also on D-Day that the 320th Barrage Balloon Battalion was employed, notable as an African American unit, its low-altitude balloons part of the air-defenses over Utah and Omaha beaches. Not only was it the only American barrage balloon battalion employed in the invasion, it was also the only black unit to come ashore on D-Day. This battalion, later cited for their courage and bravery by General Eisenhower, was under heavy fire from German artillery determined to cut their balloons adrift, but their five battalion medics also worked hard amidst the carnage on Omaha Beach to tend to the wounded, including Corporal Waverly Woodson, Jr. He treated at least 200 soldiers and saved four from drowning after being wounded while first wading ashore under heavy fire. He was later nominated for the Medal of Honor, but it was never awarded, not surprising as no black soldier would ever gain our nation's highest award for valor during the war because of the discrimination they faced. In this ad, the chemical giant Shell highlights the use of its petroleum products to make these balloons hold their helium.

5

Naval Fighters, Bombers, and Patrol Aircraft

Naval aircraft gained their fair share of advertising publicity during the war, though not to the same extent that U.S. Army aircraft did. Most publicized, of course, were the Navy fighters, especially the Grumman Wildcat and Hellcat; though, the famed and important Corsair, curiously enough, was little advertised overall. Dive-bombing aircraft and patrol planes also received a lesser share of attention, not surprisingly, though, once again, Grumman's Avenger was an exception, as was the Martin Mariner Flying boat. Among the biggest advertisers for Navy aircraft were the big tire companies, B. F. Goodrich and Goodyear, not surprising as they were both major suppliers, or, in the case of Goodyear, contract builders. The letter designations for these aircraft are as follows: F for fighters, SB for scout bombers, TB for torpedo bombers, PV for patrol aircraft, PB for patrol bombers, and OS for observation scout planes. Additional letters and numbers refer to the manufacturer of the aircraft (SBD Dauntless meaning a scout bomber made by Douglas) and later design models.

Fighter Aircraft

Brewster F2A Buffalo

This tubby little fighter played an interesting role during the war. First conceived in 1935, it was even chosen over the Grumman Wildcat as the fighter of choice, a bad mistake as hindsight would show. This was also the first plane that Brewster ever built. The fighter, the Navy's first ever monoplane, was only 26 feet long with a 35-foot wingspan, and was armed with four machine guns. Only 509 were ever built and the Brewster factory was plagued with management and strike problems during the war, eventually taken over by the government. The Buffalo, sadly, was obsolete before the war even began, and performed badly in the Pacific during its limited time in service, being nicknamed the "flying coffin." It was overweight, slow, and no match for the Japanese Zero fighter. The Buffalo was used by a number of other nations, including the British and, most notably, Finland. It first saw American service during the Battle of Midway, where a mixed force of six Wildcats and twenty Buffalos, led by Major Floyd Parks, intercepted a Japanese raid on the island. Thirteen out of twenty Buffalos were shot down, including Parks plane, he being strafed and killed after bailing out of his burning fighter. After this, the few remaining Buffalos were sent back to the U.S. to be used as training aircraft. Curiously, it was the Finnish Air Force that used the Brewster fighter to great effect in their fight with the Soviets from 1941–1944. During that conflict, thirty-six of their pilots became aces, the leader achieving thirty-nine kills. The fighter was found to be easy to fly, and was much easier to maintain in the cold weather, unlike in the Pacific, and the Finnish tactics were never solved by the Soviets. Because of their success, the Buffalo cannot be ignored, it having the highest number of aces produced in ratio with the number of planes built, which just illustrates that old adage, that "one man's trash is another man's treasure." The aircraft company that produced this ad once made their own aircraft, but by the Depression was manufacturing metal pots and pans; during World War II, its workforce, expanded to over 5,000 employees, was supplying exhaust manifolds for Navy warplanes.

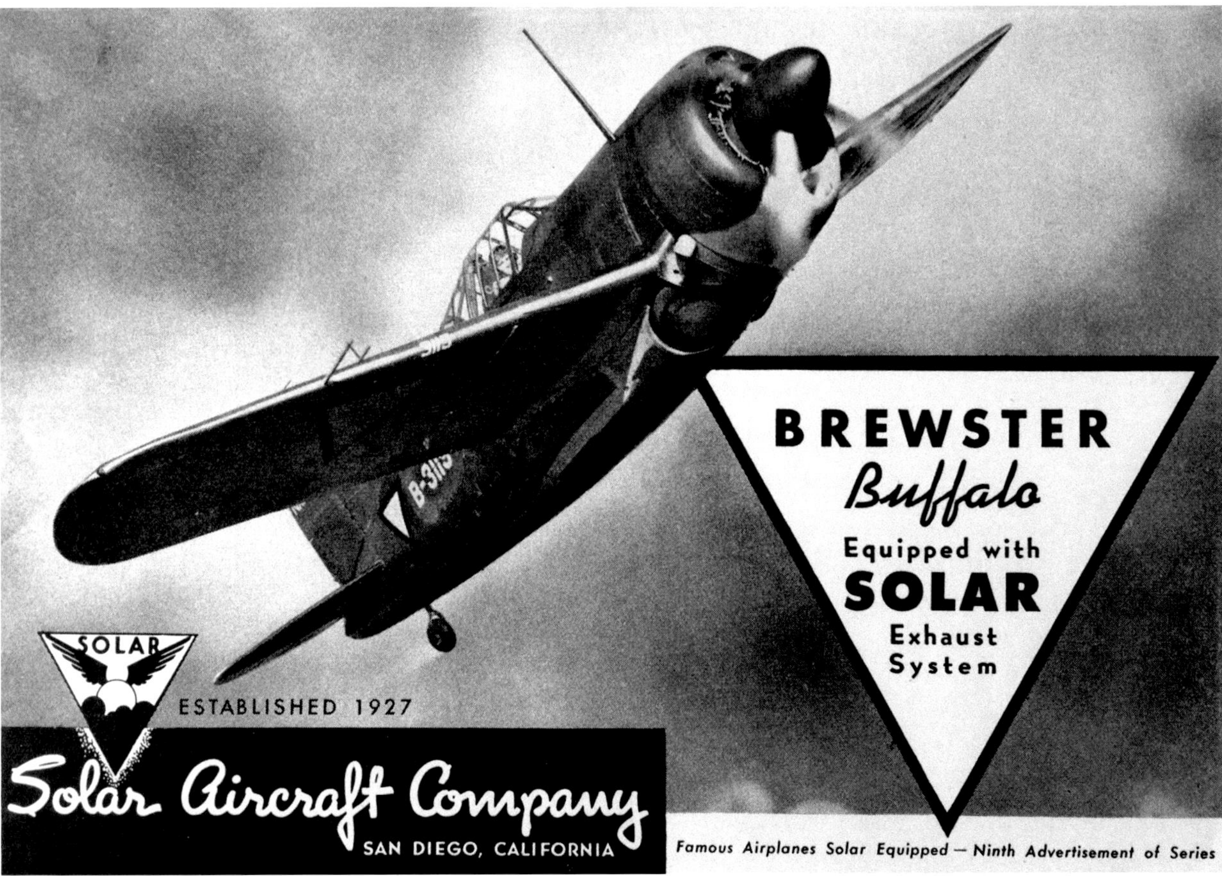

GRUMMAN F4F WILDCAT

This carrier-based fighter was one of the most important fighters of the war, used by the U.S., as well as the RAF and the Canadians, with nearly 8,000 built. It was first designed in 1935, but when the original design was shown to be inferior to the Brewster Buffalo, Grumman designers went back to the drawing board to make improvements. As a result, the fighter was not only ordered by the U.S. in small numbers, but also by the French. Because France fell to the Germans before they could be delivered, their order went to Britain, they naming their version the Martlet. The fighter was officially adopted by the U.S. Navy just over two months before Pearl Harbor, with production ramped up after the Brewster Buffalo proved itself a failure. The accepted version could fly at a speed of 325 mph and was armed with six machine guns, two in each wing and two in the fuselage. The fighter was also equipped to carry two 250-lb. bombs under the wings. Though outclassed by the Japanese Zero fighter, the Wildcat was a rugged plane which, fighting with special tactics, held the line in the Pacific until the F6F Hellcat and F4U Corsair arrived on the scene. The Wildcat saw its first combat with the Royal Navy's Fleet Air Arm, shooting down a German bomber off Scapa Flow in December 1940, while in September 1941, serving aboard the carrier HMS *Audacity*, six Martlets shot down several big Focke-Wulf Condor bombers during convoy escort operations. This role as an escort carrier fighter, both with the Royal Navy and the U.S. Navy, would be one of the Wildcat's premier achievements of the war. Later, with the U.S. Navy in the Pacific, the Wildcat fought well at Wake Island in December 1941, and was a key weapon in the Guadalcanal campaign while operating from land bases. In all, the Grumman F4F Wildcat manned by Navy and Marine pilots flew some 15,500 sorties during the war, over 14,000 from the deck of an aircraft carrier. The B. F. Goodrich ad shown here highlights the company's role as a primary tire supplier for Navy aircraft.

GRUMMAN F6F HELLCAT

This carrier-based fighter, first developed beginning in 1942 based on the experiences of Grumman Wildcat fighters, was one of the Navy's mainstay fighters in the second half of the war. Prototypes first flew in mid-1942, but by early 1943, operational Hellcat units began to appear, first aboard the carrier USS *Essex*. The Hellcat

The B.F. Goodrich
Airplane of the month
GRUMMAN "WILDCAT"
"WILDCATS" OVER WAKE ISLAND made history for the Marine Corps . . . as they did west of the Gilberts for the Navy. This Grumman F4F pursuit ship, which can be either carrier- or land-based, has already won its service stripes in Democracy's battle. B. F. Goodrich supplies the "Wildcat" with Silvertown tires for safer, smoother landings whether on the pitching deck of an aircraft carrier or on a shell-torn military field. Grumman has long been making fine ships for our Navy and so this month B. F. Goodrich salutes Grumman, maker of the fast F4F pursuit known as the "Wildcat."
The Navy flies with
B.F.Goodrich
FIRST IN RUBBER

Grumman
U. S. Navy's Grumman Night Fighters Hit Tokyo
F6F-5N Grumman Hellcats
Grumman
AIRCRAFT ENGINEERING CORPORATION, Bethpage, L. I., N. Y.

was powered by a Pratt & Whitney Double Wasp radial engine, faster than the Wildcat by 50 mph, and was armed with six Browning machine guns, and able to carry a 2,000-lb. bomb load, as well as attachments for six rockets under the wings. The Hellcat was produced in incredible numbers, some 12,300 built in all, including 11,000 in 1942–44 alone. The fighter's success was immediately felt, it soon gaining mastery over the Japanese as it was faster than the Zero. Despite their late entry into the war, Hellcats accounted for about 75 percent of all aerial victories achieved by the U.S. Navy during the entire war, most sorties flown from carriers. This superiority was demonstrated early on in operations over Tarawa in November 1943, where thirty Zero fighters were destroyed with only one Hellcat lost. Not surprisingly, the Navy's top ace, Captain David McCampbell, achieved all of his thirty-four kills in the fighter. After the war, the Navy's Blue Angels flight demonstration team chose a Hellcat variant as their first aircraft. Though phased out of the Navy's arsenal after the Korean War, foreign navies continued to fly the Hellcat up to 1960. This interesting ad from Grumman dates from 1945 and highlights the night-fighter version of the Hellcat, which was painted black and carried a wing-mounted radar pod, as depicted here. The mention of hitting Tokyo likely references a February 1945 raid made by carrier-based dive-bombers escorted by Hellcats which took place over two days, resulting in the loss of over 500 Japanese aircraft, against the loss of eighty American planes.

Vought F4U Corsair

Called by aviation historian Bill Gunston "one of the greatest combat aircraft in history," the Corsair was the first American fighter to exceed the speed of 400 mph. Answering the Navy's call for a maximum speed fighter, a prototype was first built in 1938, with a further developed fighter produced in 1940. The Corsair was faster and bigger than any other Navy fighter and had the largest propeller. Though the first production model was delivered in 1942, the Corsair was an entirely new beast, and one difficult to fly with some problems yet to be worked out. In addition to Vought, Corsairs were also built by Goodyear, as well as at the Navy-operated Brewster plant. The fighter first saw combat in February 1943 with the Marine Corps, flying from land bases in

the Solomon Islands. Carrier operations for the Corsair, distinguished by its unusual gull-winged configuration, were also tried, but proved to be problematic and the fighter was subsequently assigned to land-based Marine Corps units, where many aces would soon emerge. Among them were Major Gregory "Pappy" Boyington, leader of the famed Black Sheep Squadron (VMF-214), who achieved twenty-two kills in the Corsair. Interestingly, because of the unusual air intake slots located on the wings of the Corsair, it was nicknamed "Whistling Death" by their Japanese opponents for the sound it made at high speed. The big Corsair was also very adept in the fighter-bomber role, playing a key role at Iwo Jima and Okinawa. So good was the Corsair that it achieved a kill ratio of over eleven to one, with 189 of them lost while flying over 64,000 sorties. Even after the war, production of the Corsair continued up to 1952, with some 12,500 being built overall, the fighter playing a key role during the Korean War in a ground attack role. This ad from Nash-Kelvinator highlights the Pratt & Whitney "super-charged" engines made by the company for the Corsair.

Torpedo and Dive Bombers

Curtiss SB2C Helldiver

This aptly-named carrier-based dive bomber was probably the most successful dive bomber of the war for the Allies, at least on a technical level, but this success took over two years to arrive. Developed as a replacement for the Douglas Dauntless, the Helldiver began to take form in 1939, but because of the many changes requested by the Navy, as well as the crash of several prototypes, full-scale production did not begin until mid-1942, with the first aircraft reaching the front lines in November 1943. Initial results were, however, unfavorable, so the Navy and Curtiss had to go back to the drawing board, the major change being a switch to the Wright Twin-Cyclone engine, and a four-bladed propeller, both of which solved the power problem. With these modifications, the Helldiver showed her form beginning in 1944 during operations over the Marianas, the Philippines, Iwo Jima, and Okinawa, and sinking Japan's two largest battleships. Overall, some 7,200 Helldivers were built during the war, but the dive bomber was soon thereafter, in 1947, relegated to reserve units, and was finally retired from service in 1950. This ad from the bomber's manufacturer likely highlights its raids on the Japanese capital in February 1945 (see the Grumman Hellcat above).

Douglas SBD Dauntless

This distinguished dive bomber played a major part in the role in the crucial early years, and overall sank more tons of Japanese shipping than any other Allied aircraft. The bomber was first developed by the Northrup company, and continued under Douglas when they took over that company in 1937. Production began in 1939, with first units going to the Marines in 1940 and the Navy in early 1941, with nearly 6,000 built overall until production ended in 1944. The most successful version of the Dauntless, which carried a two-man crew, was powered by a Wright Cyclone radial engine and capable of carrying up to a 1,500-lb. bomb load. The bomber was capable of a maximum speed of 250 mph, well-armed with two machine guns in the nose and two fired from the rear cockpit, and is best recognized for the perforated dive brakes on the wings. From the very beginning of the war, the SBD Dauntless made its mark, with aircraft from the carrier USS *Enterprise* sinking a Japanese submarine on December 10, 1941, while in May 1942, during the Battle of the Coral Sea, a force of twenty-four SBDs from the carrier USS *Yorktown* attacked the Japanese carrier *Shokaku*. While many pilots missed their mark, Lt. John Powers and his radioman Everett Hill made it through, the wing of their bomber on fire after being hit by a Zero fighter, and dropped a bomb dead center on the carrier's flight deck, badly damaging the ship and putting her out of the war for months. The SBD subsequently crashed alongside the carrier, killing Powers and Hill, with Powers being awarded the Medal of Honor for his bravery. In that same battle, the first sinking ever of an aircraft carrier occurred when SBDs of USS *Lexington* attacked and sank the Japanese carrier *Shoho*, resulting in the famed radio message "Scratch one flat top" from the squadron commander. This was just the first carrier kill for the Dauntless, as the aircraft changed the course of the war just a month later. At the Battle of Midway in June 1942, Dauntless aircraft from USS *Enterprise* and USS *Yorktown* sank the Japanese carriers *Soryu*, *Hiryu*, *Kaga*, and *Akagi*, thereby turning the tide in the Pacific in one of the most epic naval battles in history. This ad from a famed motor-oil brand almost certainly portrays a Dauntless attack at Midway.

Douglas TBD Devastator

At the time of its conception in 1935, this three-seater torpedo bomber was the first monoplane designed for such a role. Though a good airplane in its day, by the beginning of World War II the torpedo bomber was

HELLDIVERS HIT TOKYO

Tokyo has now felt the Navy's new pile-driving punch. It's the carrier-borne Curtiss SB2C-4, latest in an already famed line of sluggers, and it lugs one of the greatest loads of destructive power ever mounted in a naval aircraft.

Ominously termed "The Beast" by flight crews, this potent dive-bomber retains the speed, range and climbing power of its Helldiver predecessors — yet — here is its inventory of death-dealing weapons. Two 20 mm wing cannons! 1000 pounds of bombs on wing racks! Better than 1000 pounds of fuselage bomb load! Eight 5 inch rockets! Two flexible machine guns!

Watch the reports from our Pacific Fleet and you'll know why the Japs watch the skies with fear and trembling. "The Beast" has a mission. It's to raise Hell with the Sons of Heaven.

Says an official Navy release, "The Helldiver . . . now our dive-bomber . . . has proved its worth time and time again in the Pacific campaign." Chances are several million bombed, blasted, rocketed residents of Japan will readily agree!

Here's one great advantage the Axis can't match...

"THE PENNSYLVANIA PLUS"*

**The big margin of superiority Nature gave to Pennsylvania grade crude oil*

In that last 30 seconds of a dog fight . . . in that blinding pull-out of a dive-bomber . . . our flyers know that Pennsylvania oils add a positive superiority to engine performance.

These oils give a flyer the edge, with a superiority as definite and as outstanding as the superiority of the U. S. bomb-sight.

All the conquests of the aggressor nations have given them no lubricants comparable to those produced from Pennsylvania grade crude oil. And no synthetic substitutes even remotely approach Nature's greatest contribution to the lubrication of war machines...lubricants made from this same Pennsylvania grade crude oil.

Quaker State, for many years a leader in this quality field, refines this Pennsylvania crude with long-acquired skill . . . with the most modern equipment . . . with the most advanced processes. These Quaker State oils are going into the war, spreading the fighting film of Pennsylvania molecules inside many types of engines . . . molecules that no motor can tear apart, and no Axis scientist can put together. Quaker State Oil Refining Corp., Oil City, Pa.

QUAKER STATE MOTOR OIL

Retail price 35¢ per quart

STABILIZED QUAKER STATE MOTOR OIL

75

outdated. The crew included a pilot, radio operator, and a gunner, the big bomber was slow and heavy with little armored protection for the crew, armed with two machine guns and capable of carrying a single torpedo, as well as an additional 500-lb. bomb load. In the first months of the war, the Devastator performed well in action in the Marshall Islands and attacking Japanese shipping in New Guinea, flying off the decks of the carriers USS *Enterprise*, USS *Yorktown*, and USS *Lexington*. During the Battle of the Coral Sea, the Devastator had mixed results, helping to sink the Japanese carrier *Shoho*, but performing poorly in their attack on *Shokaku*. Though it is likely this mixed performance was due to the defective torpedoes the bomber was carrying, the Devastator would meet her final end a month later in June 1942 during the Battle of Midway. In this battle, while the newer SBD Dauntless hit its targets, the Devastator itself was devastated; all fifteen of the Devastators of Torpedo Squadron 8 from USS *Hornet* were shot down while attacking the Japanese carrier fleet, with only one man, Ensign George Gay, out of the thirty crewmen involved surviving. Likewise, nine of the fourteen Devastators from USS *Enterprise* and ten out of twelve from USS *Yorktown* were shot down, none obtaining hits. While the Devastator attacks and lack of hits were once again due, at least in part, to defective torpedoes, and while the Devastator attacks did serve as a distraction, the end was at hand. This would be the last combat for this now obsolete bomber, with surviving aircraft subsequently withdrawn from service. Of the 130 total Devastators that were built, only thirty-nine remained, they given over to training duties, with none remaining in the Navy's inventory by 1945. Today, unlike many examples of World War II aircraft, there are no surviving examples, though the wreck sites of some are known. Because the Devastator was obsolete by the beginning of the war and had such low production numbers, advertisements for this aircraft, like that for components supplier White-Rodgers, are relatively few in number.

Grumman TBF Avenger

Just as the Douglas Devastator saw the end of its life at the Battle of Midway in June 1942, the Grumman Avenger, designed as its replacement, saw its first action there in a limited role. Its design accepted in 1940, the first Avenger was built in 1941, and the first aircraft to enter service were delivered in January 1942. This three-man torpedo bomber was the heaviest single-engined aircraft of the war, weighing in at 10,100 lb. empty, and distinguished by its folding wings and the rear facing electrically operated turret in some models. The crew consisted of a pilot, radioman/bombardier, and a turret gunner. Interestingly, the pilot's cockpit was inaccessible by the other crewmen. The Avenger was a good performer, but had an inauspicious start, with five of the six Avengers flying from Midway Island being shot down, the other badly damaged. However, things would improve as Navy pilots became more familiar with the aircraft, and just several months later Avengers from USS *Saratoga* and USS *Enterprise* sank the Japanese carrier *Ryujo* in the Eastern Solomons, while just a few months later, in November 1942, they helped sink the battleship *Hiei* during the Naval Battle of Guadalcanal. From this time to the end of the war, the aptly-named Avenger gained her fair share of revenge against the Japanese, sinking another carrier and two battleships. However, the Avenger was not just deadly to enemy surface ships, it was also an effective submarine killer, credited with downing thirty Japanese submarines. The Avenger also saw carrier duty in the Atlantic and served effectively in that theatre as well. Notable Avenger fliers including future President George H. W. Bush, whose plane was shot down off Chichi Jima in 1944, and future actor Paul Newman, who served as an Avenger rear gunner. Interestingly, it was the disappearance of a flight of five Avengers that went missing while on a training mission off the Florida coast in late 1945 that contributed to the legend of the Bermuda Triangle. Even after the war, the Avenger continued in service into the 1950s before its final retirement. This ad not only highlights the fact that Pesco built components for the Avenger, but the artist's representation certainly depicts one its first battle actions against a Japanese carrier, here identified with a big red sun on the flight deck in unrealistic fashion.

Patrol and Scout Aircraft

Consolidated PBY Catalina

This flying boat type of patrol bomber aircraft, one of several models built by Consolidated, was one of the most useful aircraft to see service during the war. With about 4,000 Catalinas built, it was also the largest production run ever for any flying boat in history. The aircraft, noted for its parasol-style wing configuration, was conceived beginning in the early 1930s, with the first prototype in the air by 1935, and the first Catalinas arriving in Navy squadrons

To concentrate on
IGHTING POWER
White-Rodgers offers entirely new developments in automatic temperature modulation equipment for the control of —
1. ENGINE COWL FLAPS (BOTH AIR AND LIQUID COOLED).
2. OIL COOLER SHUTTERS OR FLAPS.
3. CABIN TEMPERATURE (BOTH SUPER-CHARGED AND NORMAL).
4. CARBURETOR AIR TEMPERATURE.
AKE THEM MORE & MORE AUTOMATIC!
WHITE-RODGERS ELECTRIC CO
SAINT LOUIS, MISSOURI

PERFORMANCE CONTROLS THE AIR
Grumman Avenger
Knockout! Down before the torpedo bomber go the mightiest heavy-weights of the enemy fleet. Through skies stark mad with defensive fire these planes close in to deliver their telling blow. A crucial test of both pilot and plane. Each torpedo striking home salutes the skill and daring of our flying sons, and craftsmanship of the millions here at home whose precision workmanship rules the sky. Pesco Products Co., 11610 Euclid Avenue, Cleveland 6, Ohio (Division Borg-Warner).
PESCO motor driven Hydraulic Pump for propeller feathering.
In Aircraft Hydraulics, Fuel Pumps, Air Pumps, Related Accessories...
PERFORMANCE POINTS TO Pesco FIRST

in late 1936. Interestingly, the name for the aircraft was coined by the British, who had ordered thirty of them in 1941, it being named after California's Santa Catalina Island. This big and ungainly-looking aircraft, measuring 63 feet long and with a wingspan of 104 feet, was manned by a seven- to ten-man crew and was powered by two Pratt & Whitney Twin Wasp radial engines. The Catalina, sadly, was slow, and though armed with four machine guns (including one each in its distinctive waist "blisters"), was easy to shoot down. Nonetheless, the Catalina's great versatility overrode these problems. It was excellent as an air-sea rescue boat (in which service they were nicknamed "Dumbo") and saved countless numbers of downed airmen and sailors, including fifty-six men from the sunken cruiser USS *Indianapolis* in 1945, and continued in this capacity well after the war ended. Its role as a patrol aircraft was also legendary and with a range of over 3,000 miles, it could patrol a lot of airspace. It was a Navy PBY that found the Japanese fleet at the outset of the Battle of Midway, while it was an RAF Catalina that discovered the German battleship *Bismarck*. Yet another specialty of the Catalina was anti-submarine work, especially during the Battle of the Atlantic, where Catalinas flown by RAF Coastal Command, the RCAF (they naming the PBY the Canso), the U.S. Navy, as well as those operated by the Brazilian and Norwegian navies combined to sink about forty German U-boats. Finally, the Catalina was also a noted combat aircraft, employed by the U.S. Navy and the RAAF as a nighttime raider, employed in attacking enemy shipping, bombing Japanese bases, laying mines, as well as performing rescue missions. The most noted of these combat units were the Black Cat Squadrons of the U.S. Navy, they first being employed during the Guadalcanal campaign in 1942. The Cats of these squadrons, about fourteen in all, were equipped with radar and were painted a matte black color to aid in their stealth missions. Soon enough, they came to be feared by the Japanese and were actively hunted themselves. Catalinas remained in use by the U.S. Navy up to 1957, but were used by foreign air forces well into the 1970s. This ad by the Catalina's maker not only highlights its combat role, but also, quite strangely and humorously, includes a "safety" vignette featuring a plane crash.

Consolidated PB2Y Coronado

First developed in 1937, the Coronado was a result of the U.S. Navy's plans for a more modern patrol bomber but fell far short of that mark. Being 79 feet long and with a 115-foot wingspan, powered by four Pratt & Whitney Twin Wasp radial engines, the Coronado was a big aircraft, used by the Navy in a limited combat role as a bomber and anti-submarine aircraft in the last year and a half of the war. However, their short range, less than half that of the Catalina, made the PB2Y suited for little more than transport duties, and only 217 were ever built, with a small amount being used by the RAF. By 1946, most of the surviving Coronado PB2Ys were scrapped, and only one remains in existence today. The nice color ad for this aircraft was part of a monthly series put out by B. F. Goodrich, who built some of its components.

Consolidated PB4Y-2 Privateer

Yet another patrol bomber built by the Consolidated Aircraft Company of San Diego, the Privateer came about as a result of their famed B-24 Liberator design. Many mistake the Privateer as a converted Liberator due to their similar appearance, but in fact it was a completely different aircraft in most aspects. Development began in early 1943 when several B-24 airframes were converted. In the end, the many changes in the airframe and design of the Privateer resulted in a new aircraft altogether. Though the revolutionary Davis wing configuration was retained, the fuselage of the Privateer was 7 feet longer and, most notably the tail assembly was changed, the oval-slabbed stabilizers of the B-24 replaced with a large vertical tail. Because this new design was much heavier than the B-24, the PB4Y-2 was also slower. The Privateer was also more heavily armed than the Liberator, primarily designed as a low-level bomber. Between 1944 and 1945, 739 Privateers were built, most at the war's end, and their wartime service was limited. After the war, they were employed on nighttime missions in the Korean War, and during the early years of the Cold War patrolled close to the Soviet coast in Eastern Europe, with one Privateer being shot down in 1950 over the Baltic Sea. The Privateer was phased out of the U.S. Air Force by 1954, though used by the Coast Guard up to 1958. Some Privateers were used as civilian aerial firefighting aircraft, the last used in this capacity in the U.S. in 2002. This ad by Koppers gives an excellent profile view of the Privateer and the large tail fin which distinguished it from the B-24.

Lockheed PV1 Ventura/PV2 Harpoon

This Navy patrol bomber was a successor to Lockheed's very successful Hudson bomber (see above), first developed in 1940, and was based on their civilian

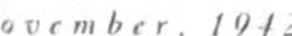

21

Dive Bomber—?

19 years of technical skill and engineering ingenuity are built into the Consolidated PBY patrol bomber . . . the Catalina.

We think she's the finest plane of her type in the world. But even with our intimate knowledge of her ruggedness and fine design, we were unprepared for a recent message that came in from "Down Under":

"Catalinas have actually engaged in dive bombing, in defiance of their designer's aims!"

. . .

Consolidated Aircraft Corporation, San Diego, California. Member, Aircraft War Production Council, Inc.

Reproduced in the interest of safety, by permission of the Army Air Corps.

CONSOLIDATED® builds Battleships of the Air

®Originator of the LIBERATOR . . . CATALINA . . . CORONADO

Navy's new long-range bomber uses American Hammered piston rings

This is the "Privateer," sea-going sister of the Army's Liberator. Like so many other Navy and Army planes, it has American Hammered Piston Rings. Because of the efficient chrome plating process used by this Koppers division, the armed forces were able to reduce their aircraft piston ring requirements by millions of rings. The Porus-Krome (Van der Horst process) wearing surface doubled and redoubled piston ring life and tripled cylinder life.

Roofing with Coal Tar Pitch

Old Style Pitch and Approved Tarred Felt produced by the Tar and Chemical Division of Koppers have been used on many of the large airplane factories and on many airport structures.

Aviation Tidewater Structures are Pressure-Treated

This landing dock and many other aviation structures are built with wood pressure-treated to resist decay and the attacks of marine borers and termites. Koppers Wood Preserving Division pressure-treats wood for this and other purposes.

Buy VICTORY BONDS . . . and keep them!

KOPPERS COMPANY, INC.

PITTSBURGH 19, PA.

KOPPERS

THE INDUSTRY THAT SERVES ALL INDUSTRY

Lodestar Transport liner. It is often called the Vega Ventura as it was built by Vega Aircraft, a subsidiary of Lockheed, and was first used by the RAF as a medium bomber in 1942. Though built as a bigger aircraft than the Hudson, with more powerful engines, the Ventura proved a failure on bombing raids over Europe because it was too vulnerable without fighter escort. As a result, most RAF Venturas were transferred to their Coastal Command. The vast majority of the 1,600 PV1s built were used by the U.S. Navy, with a redesigned version appearing in early 1944 and named the Harpoon. The PV1 first saw combat in February 1943 in the Aleutians, with some even equipped as night-fighters and used in the Solomon Islands. Like so many other warbirds, the Ventura and Harpoon were quickly retired from military service after the war's end and scrapped. This ad by Lockheed was one of a series early in the war which showed their aircraft with RAF roundels rather than American insignia.

Martin PBM Mariner

This large twin-engined flying boat was the largest of its type ever built and was a very successful patrol bomber during the war. The Mariner was developed by the Glenn L. Martin Company beginning in 1937 and first entered production in 1939. It had a range of over 3,000 miles and could carry up to a 4,000-lb. bomb load. The Mariner first entered service with the U.S. Navy in 1940 and even before the beginning of the war was employed in patrolling the waters of the North Atlantic from Iceland, along with the Catalina. In February 1942, the Mariner flown by CMDR. Richard Schreder sank the first of ten U-boats Mariners would destroy during the war, depth-charging *U-158* off Bermuda. The Mariner was also heavily used during operations in the Pacific, serving as a patrol bomber, transport, and air-sea rescue craft. Like the Catalina, Mariners were also used in a combat role, with some "Nightmare" Squadrons flying black-painted Mariners that made nighttime attacks on Japanese shipping and bases. The Martin PBM Mariner was built in smaller numbers than the Catalina, 1,366 in all, and though it was considered to be a superior patrol bomber, it would never gain the publicity and fame of the Catalina. It is perhaps for this reason that the Mariner was heavily advertised during the war, mostly by Martin themselves, as shown here. This ad is also interesting for its recruitment aspect and its pitch for young men to join the "Navy Air Force."

Vought OS2U Kingfisher

This observation scout-plane was carried aboard battleships and cruisers of the U.S. Navy during the war. It was launched by catapult and distinguished by its large central float and two wing-mounted stabilizing floats. First designed in 1938, the Kingfisher entered service in late 1940. Though not designed as a combat aircraft, it was nonetheless armed with two machine guns and capable of carrying two small bombs or depth charges. The Kingfisher operated with a pilot and a radioman/gunner, though some Kingfishers did operate from land-based airfields, including those operated by 107 Squadron of the RAAF from 1943–45. While the Kingfisher was slow, it was a rugged aircraft and performed a variety of tasks during the war, including rescuing downed airmen (including forty operated by the U.S. Coast Guard), as well as anti-submarine duties where, in July 1942 off Cape Hatteras, two Kingfishers providing air cover for a coastal convoy destroyed *U-576* with the assistance of USS *Unicoi*. In rare cases, the Kingfisher even engaged enemy aircraft, with one OS2U downing a Japanese Zero fighter off Iwo Jima in February 1945. Overall, just over 1,500 Kingfishers were built, it being gradually phased out of service beginning in late 1944. This ad by Edo documents the fight in which an OS2U shot down a Zero.

"Ventura" – the Hudson's brother in defense

Across the warways of the world wings a new bomber–the Vega Ventura, big brother to the Hudson...the peacetime Lodestar transport redesigned for war.

Greater in bomb-carrying capacity and range... faster... more formidable in fire power than the Hudson, the Ventura again shows vividly the soundness of American engineering. Adapted... like the Hudson... from a commercial design, this internationally famous transport for trade has become a bomber for democracy.

Lockheed and its affiliate, Vega, work hand in hand for defense. In a new, streamlined-for-speed plant, eager Vega craftsmen are now swinging into Ventura production that will soon match the record of the Hudson.

... for Protection today and Progress tomorrow

Lockheed

LEADER IN PRODUCTION

Figures available for the first half of 1941 show:

LOCKHEED produced the greatest dollar volume of planes in American aviation industry.

LOCKHEED produced more two-engine aircraft than any other American manufacturer ... Hudson Bombers ... Lightning P-38 Interceptors and Transports.

TODAY... Lockheed and Vega employ over 50,000 craftsmen ... more than any other organization in airplane production.

LOOK TO *Lockheed* FOR LEADERSHIP

THREE REASONS WHY *The Martin Mariner* IS POISON TO U-BOATS!

THE Navy is frequently silent on sub-sinkings. But when you read of convoy after convoy getting through, you know Martin Mariners are at work. From Iceland to Rio these big 20-ton flying boats help guard the sea lanes, ready at a moment's notice to unleash a storm of gunfire and depth charges on lurking killers of the deep. They're deadly poison to U-boats!

WHY MARINERS ARE TOPS AGAINST SUBS

Take a look at the picture above and note the big sturdy hull. That means seaworthiness, the ability to take off or land in rough weather, maintaining the constant, never-ceasing hunt for U-boats. Then look at the broad tail with its twin fins. That gives stability, a steady platform, assured accuracy in bombing. Finally, there's the spread of those long, gull-wings. Such wingspread enables Mariners to "coast" through the air, with engines throttled down for minimum fuel consumption, permitting them to stay aloft hours longer. In addition, these tough PBM's pack sufficient fire-power to slug it out with a U-boat's guns when making low-level attacks. The Mariner was designed as a scourge for subs!

YOUR OWN COMMAND

When you pilot a Martin Mariner, you're leader of an eleven-man crew. If you've got what it takes to fly, you belong in the Navy Air Force. It's a real opportunity to learn the trade of the future . . . aviation. Even now Martin has completed plans for giant 150-ton "flying hotels," the transportation of tomorrow. Such ships, weaving an aerial network over the world will require crews of expert fliers. You can be one of them, if you start now to win your Navy Wings of Gold!

THE GLENN L. MARTIN COMPANY
BALTIMORE-3, MARYLAND
The Glenn L. Martin-Nebraska Company—Omaha

OFFICIAL NAVY PHOTOS SHOW MARTIN MARINERS SINKING NAZI SUB

BOMBS AWAY! Strings of depth charges cascade from Mariner's bays. Extra-big bomb capacity enables Mariner to drop lethal patterns of explosives blanketing target area.

DIRECT HITS! Straddled by depth charges, sub is forced to surface, crippled. Twin tail fins, assuring stability, permit accurate bombing like this, make Mariners the scourge of subs.

HELPLESS! Unable to submerge or flee, U-boat lies helpless. Mariner, designed to stay aloft for very long periods, circles watchfully until destroyer arrives to polish off the sub.

IN a recent engagement against Jap-occupied *Iwo Jima*, a KINGFISHER Observation Scout Seaplane (OS2U) had been catapulted off a United States cruiser to direct Naval gunfire.

Circling over the island in full view of an enemy airfield, Lieutenant Robert W. Hendershott, U.S.N.R., of Bend, Oregon, pilot of the lightly armed little float plane, calmly proceeded to fulfill his hazardous but vitally important mission.

The slow-cruising Kingfisher looked like an easy mark to the Nip's nest of Zero fighters. Hardly had the surface vessels begun their bombardment, when Hendershott's Observer, Arthur E. Hickman, Aviation Radioman, second class, U.S.N.R., of Denver, Colorado, spotted three Zeros spiralling up.

Rapidly gaining altitude, the enemy planes opened fire on the Kingfisher from below. The lead attacker made a stern approach. Hickman, crouching over his light machine gun, coolly bided his time, and as the fast, heavily armed Zero came within range, let go with a perfectly aimed burst into its engine.

Hickman's bullets must have killed the Jap pilot. For the Zero roared on in—sheared off the Kingfisher's starboard wing tip—and crashed into the sea.

The second Zero came on. Its bullets ripped through the Kingfisher's fuselage within inches of the Navy pilot's legs. The oil tank was punctured. Hot oil spurted over the windshield and cockpit.

Again and again, the two fast and highly maneuverable Jap fighters slammed at the crippled Kingfisher. The fuselage was completely riddled. Finally, Pilot Hendershott maneuvered his plane within reach of the protecting screen of U. S. destroyers and cruisers—and the Jap fliers pulled away!

Score: One Edo float equipped Navy Seaplane damaged. One latest-type Zero knocked into the sea. Two other Zeros badly baffled by a non-combatant observation plane manned by two very combat-minded Navy men. The Japs should file a complaint!

EDO FLOAT GEAR

SERVES THE UNITED NATIONS

ARMY E NAVY

EDO AIRCRAFT CORPORATION

407 SECOND ST., COLLEGE POINT, L. I., N. Y.

6

Utility and Special Purpose Vehicles

A surprising number of these often less glamorous war-purposed vehicles were advertised during the war, almost certainly because they were machines that were easily recognized by the American public. Indeed, in some cases, these were militarized versions of civilian vehicles that companies like Caterpillar, Harley-Davidson, and Studebaker hoped would soon be available again on the home front. However, this was not the case for all of them, for some were vehicles that had a strictly military origin, but after the war would enter civilian use, the most notable example being the jeep. While some of these vehicle's importance, like that of the famed "Deuce and a half" cargo truck, is obvious, others, such as that of the D-7 tractor, are less so, their contributions to winning the war in workmanlike fashion largely obscured.

Allis-Chalmers M6 Artillery Tractor

This high-speed artillery tractor was based on the chassis of the M3 Light Tank and was in service beginning in 1944. The earlier M4 towed the 90-mm anti-aircraft gun, while its "big brother," as Allis-Chalmers calls it in their ad, was designed to tow heavy artillery like the 240-mm howitzer. This 38-ton monster, the biggest tractor in this series, could carry a huge load of personnel and ammunition, yet could travel up to 21 mph, enough to keep up with an armored column of vehicles. The dual compartment cab carried a driver and up to an additional nine men, while the tractor was equipped with a crane and ammunition hoist. The M6 was powered by two six-cylinder gasoline engines made by Waukesha. The M6 had as anti-aircraft protection a .50-cal. machine gun, and was involved in many combat situations, including when the Allies crossed the Rhine on the drive toward Germany in 1945. Overall, just over 1,200 of the M6, as well as over 5,000 M4s, were built by Allis-Chalmers at their plant in Springfield, Illinois, this being the first tractor plant in the country to win the Army-Navy E Award. The M4 remained in Army service until 1960.

Autocar U8144T Pontoon Semi-Tractor Truck

In order to keep Allied armies on the move in Europe from 1943 onward, lots of heavy-duty equipment and vehicles were needed to repair roads and, most importantly, rebuild bridges across major waterways like the Rhine River. These jobs were accomplished by the Army Corps of Engineers and the many combat engineer battalions that were a component of each armored and infantry division. To build the larger pontoon bridges, specially trained Heavy Pontoon Bridge Battalions were employed to get the job done. One of their major pieces of equipment was this 6-ton, 4×4 heavy tractor semi-tractor truck, built by Autocar. Some 2,700 of these trucks, the largest used by the Army, were built during the war, being powered by a Hercules RXC six-cylinder gasoline powered engine and supplied between 1941 and 1945. These trucks were of the "cab over engine" design (the driver seat located above the engine) and were adapted from a civilian-commercial model of the truck. Huge numbers of variants of this

THE BIG GUNS MOVE UP
When the giant artillery tractors begin to roll, everybody knows that something is about to happen. The big guns mean business.
This is the hour of destiny for individuals and nations—the hour when we folks back home must back our fighting men to the limit. Must show them we too are moving up—that this is *our* big push in buying War Bonds, giving blood, salvaging scrap, producing food and the machines of war.
Let's renew our determination to follow through . . . with every ounce of energy we possess. Let's *finish* the job!
WHEN YOU WRITE . . . USE V-MAIL . . . IT'S FASTER!
ALLIS-CHALMERS
TRACTOR DIVISION · MILWAUKEE 1, U. S. A.
is is the new 38-ton High Speed Tractor M-6 . . . big brother the M-4 . . . both designed and built by Allis-Chalmers cooperation with the Army Ordnance Department.

BRIDGE PARTNERS
Army Engineers and Autocar hold winning hands on many a battle-front. Mobile derricks lay ponton bridges while other special-purpose vehicles by Autocar deal a grand slam in destruction. Autocar is proud to cooperate with the Army, the Navy, the Marine Corps, and the Air Forces. Keep your own essential Autocars *rolling,* while our armed forces keep the enemy *reeling.*
AUTOCAR
MANUFACTURED IN ARDMORE, PA.
SERVICED BY FACTORY BRANCHES FROM COAST TO COAST
It's patriotic to hoard WAR BONDS

truck, outside the specialty pontoon truck, were built by Autocar and White, numbering about 11,000 in all. The winch employed on this truck for pontoon bridge building could lift 15,000 lb. and was powered by the main transmission of the truck. Some models of this truck were even equipped with a machine gun for anti-aircraft protection because, as can be seen from the ad shown here, sometimes these bridges were built while the fighting was still taking place.

Caterpillar D-7 Heavy Tractor

Few would believe that this tractor was a "weapon" that helped the Allies win the war, but military greats General Dwight D. Eisenhower and Admiral William "Bull" Halsey ranked the D-7 with the jeep, the C-47 transport, the submarine, the deuce and a half truck, and radar as machines without which the war could not have been won. That is quite the endorsement for a tractor that first appeared in 1938 and of which over 20,500 in all were built. It was the D-7 tractor, most familiar to the layman with the blade attachment that turned it into a bulldozer, which U.S. Navy Seabees (construction battalions) and U.S. Army combat engineering battalions used to build and repair roads and airstrips, as well as perform countless other construction and demolition-related tasks, including such dangerous work as clearing minefields. Manufactured by the famed Caterpillar Company of Peoria, Illinois, known for their construction yellow-painted heavy equipment, this crawler-type tractor was powered by a diesel engine, which was started by a gasoline-powered, hand-cranked motor called a "pony" motor. Incredibly, modern versions of the D-7 are still used by the Army today as its main heavy tractor. This fine ad from the end of the war describes the work of the D-7 as "bringing order out of chaos."

Dodge WC-54 Ambulance

Seldom do we think about the logistics of the aftermath of any given battle or war, but it was this 0.75-ton, 4×4 ambulance truck that transported American wounded during the war. The Dodge truck was powered by a reliable inline-six 230-cubic-inch motor with a manual four-speed transmission. Some 30,000 were built between 1942 and 1945, this ambulance able to carry a medic and four to seven patients, as well as its driver. The ambulance was equipped with a heater and folding rear step, and the sheet metal body was equipped with four foldaway bunk stretchers. The Dodge ambulance, described by its builder as a dependable vehicle of mercy, was the Army's main vehicle of this type from 1942 through the Korean War. U.S. regulations from 1942 onward specified that a bright red cross, 18 inches high, on a white background was to be displayed on each side of the vehicle with a smaller emblem, the caduceus, also painted on each side in maroon coloring. The word "ambulance" was also displayed above the windshield, flanked by a red cross. While ambulances, nicknamed "meat wagons" by their crews, were well marked according to Geneva Convention standards, both the Germans and Japanese attacked Allied medical outfits during the war on occasion.

DUKW "Duck" Amphibious Transport

This rather ungainly looking craft was actually a very unique weapon and one that proved to be extremely useful to the Allies. During World War II, invasions, whether in the Pacific, North Africa, Italy, or the rest of Europe, were all about getting a fighting army ashore. This included all the supplies such an army would need to move on from a beachhead. Unloading supply ships required, first, that a port be captured, and then required extra time to dock the ships and begin the unloading process from ship to motor-transport vehicle. But, what if, during an amphibious invasion, supplies could come ashore right with the troops and be readily available, without unloading, to move to their destination? Well, that is where the idea of the DUKW came in; these dual-purpose vehicles, which could drive on land and act like a boat in the water, could haul up to 5,000 lb. of cargo or transport twenty-four troops, and could be preloaded and ready to go in quick time. The DUKW, called a "Duck" by soldiers as a simplification of its military designation code (D=designed in 1942, U=utility vehicle, K=all wheel drive, W=dual-tandem rear axle), was designed by an American yacht-builder, a British sailor, and an engineer from MIT, and was initially rejected by the Army. However, after the DUKW rescued seven Coast Guardsmen during one of her experimental runs at Provincetown, Massachusetts, the Army changed its mind and, following other experimental tests, the vehicle was accepted and went into production and entered service in 1943. The DUKW was 31 feet long, 8 feet wide, and was manned by a single driver. About one in four DUKWs carried a machine gun, and the vehicle

Dependable Vehicles of Mercy

DOCTORS, nurses and patients know well the staunch dependability of these Dodge vehicles of mercy.

They ably perform their errands of speed or risk and they bring rescue and comfort with them wherever they go.

They can take ditches and the mudholes in their stride and they are fast as combat vehicles.

With their insulation against heat, cold, and dust, they also contain their own forced ventilation.

They have gone with the Army right to the battle fronts, and your own Dodge car or truck remains their counterpart in dependability at home.

Long before the war closed in on America, Dodge was again at its work of war production.

Dodge makes great varieties of the combat vehicles on which Army mobility depends. Also, for the Navy, Dodge makes some of the finest and most sensitive instruments of navigation to war's urgent demand...where proven craftsmanship and dependability are the only acceptable answers.

Dodge dealers, meanwhile, attend closely to their wartime responsibility of supplying essential parts and service to the millions of dependable Dodge vehicles at home.

Dodge today means *total* war production.

DIVISION OF CHRYSLER CORPORATION

[WAR BONDS ARE YOUR PERSONAL INVESTMENT IN VICTORY]

was powered by a 91-hp General Motors Model 270 straight-six engine. The vehicle was based on GMC's cab-over-engine military truck and could travel at a top speed on land of 50 mph, and 5 knots in the water. The DUKW, of which 21,000 were built from 1942–45, is considered a General Motors Company vehicle, being first built by the Yellow Truck and Coach Company, which was majority owned by General Motors in 1942, but by 1943 was wholly GMC owned. It was first used in the Pacific at Guadalcanal, but was first used in an amphibious invasion during the invasion of Sicily in July 1943, and from then on out it was a staple vehicle in any Allied landing operation. The only drawback to the DUKW was that it had no armored protection because of its sheet-metal construction, and its limitations in stormy or rough seas or when they were overloaded. This happened most notably during the D-Day landings at Omaha Beach in June 1944, where some DUKWs were overloaded with a howitzer artillery piece, several lost, along with their crews, after hitting the water from their mothership and capsizing in heavy seas. Despite this, the DUKW more than proved itself, being critical to Allied efforts to cross the Rhine River in Germany, and being equally useful in the last two years of the war in the Pacific. Because the tire pressure of the vehicle was controlled by the driver inside the cab, the DUKW could travel over coral reefs safely, and tire pressure could be changed based on operating conditions on sand or a hard-paved surface. After the war, some DUKWS were used in the Korean War, but they were soon phased out of service. Many DUKWs ended up in civilian hands, used as rescue vehicles, but they were most notably employed as tourist vehicles, the first such outfit being established at the Wisconsin Dells in 1946. To this day, despite a number of fatal accidents, so-called "Duck Boat Tours" remain a popular attraction around the country. The ad shown here features the praises of "the leading Lady of Allied landings by famed war correspondent Erne Pyle."

General Motors CCKW and Studebaker US6 2½-ton 6×6 Truck

Sometimes the simplest weapon is the most effective one, and this was certainly true during World War II in regards to the standard 2½-ton, nicknamed the "deuce and a half," cargo truck. In the modern era of warfare, the logistics of moving supplies and men from one location to another quickly and efficiently has always been the key, and the General Motors "Jimmy" truck did that for American forces in Europe. This cargo truck, known by its ordinance number G-508, was developed beginning in 1939, when the U.S. Army, with the war in Europe underway, was in search of an all-weather, all-terrain tactical truck to move men and supplies. GMC had already supplied modified commercial vehicles to the French military and their modified version of that truck resulted in the new Army truck, designated by the letters CCKW (C=designed in 1941, C=conventional cab, K=all-wheel drive, W=dual rear axles). The truck was powered by a GMC straight-six engine, capable of a top speed of about 55 mph, with a five-speed transmission and a range of 300 miles. The Jimmy was originally of a closed cab design made of metal, though some variants were built beginning in 1944 of the open cab-type with canvas roof and doors, while the standard bed had fixed sides with a drop-down tailgate, with folding seats inside the bed. The bed itself was first made of steel, but when that commodity grew scarce, a wooden bed, or a composite wood and metal bed was tried but proved unsuccessful. While the cargo truck was the most produced type of the Jimmy, there were many variants of the deuce and a half, depending on their specialized role, including those configured as dump trucks, fire trucks, fuel tankers, water tankers, and even a surgical van, among many others. In all, about 520,000 of these invaluable trucks were built by GMC, the truck being second only to the jeep in terms of production numbers during the war, and no one company produced as many vehicles of one type during the war as did GMC. It is because of these numbers, of course, that when it comes to the war in Europe, where they were most used, this truck was ubiquitous. The Army Transportation Corps employed the Jimmys in their hundreds of truck companies to keep the army supplied, but the need for supplies became most acute during the last year of the war and the Allied drive toward Germany. Moving at quick speed, the Allied divisions needed to be continually supplied and as the supply lines, first from the Normandy beachhead, grew longer, so too did the need for more truck companies rapidly increase. The Allied drive slowed, not due to enemy resistance, but because tanks and other vehicles needed more gas, quickly. Thus, it came about that the Red Ball Express was formed beginning in late August 1944. During the time of its operation, from August–November 1944, over 6,000 trucks carried over 400,000 tons of supplies to the advancing American Army. Since the Army Transportation Corp did not have enough transportation companies and trucks,

TREMENDOUS
CHEVROLET
U.S.A.
CANADA
U.S.S.R.
GERMANY
POLAND
FRANCE
TURKEY
ALGERIA
LIBYA

PRODUCTION

Meets a Tremendous Worldwide Transportation Problem

4x2 MILITARY TRUCKS

4x4 MILITARY TRUCKS

6x6 MILITARY TRUCKS

CHEVROLET TRUCKS, "thrift-carriers for the nation" in time of peace, are "victory-carriers for the nation" in time of war.

They are serving our distinguished officers and men on battlefronts all over the world with the same rugged stamina and dependability which have always characterized their performance at home.

Chevrolet has been supplying the armed forces with huge numbers of these vitally important land transports, month after month, since long before Pearl Harbor.

It has built and delivered scores of thousands of 4x4 military trucks (four-wheelers with all wheels driven)—additional thousands of 4x2's (four-wheelers with rear-wheel drive) . . . and it has made equally impressive contributions to the nation's production of 6x6 military trucks (six-wheeled vehicles with six wheels driven).

It takes tremendous production of all these units to meet America's tremendous worldwide transportation problem; and Chevrolet—largest builder of trucks in peacetime—is doing its full share to meet this need as part of its program of VOLUME FOR VICTORY.

Every Sunday Afternoon, GENERAL MOTORS SYMPHONY OF THE AIR, NBC Network

BUY WAR BONDS
SPEED THE VICTORY

CHEVROLET DIVISION OF GENERAL MOTORS

AKING PRATT & WHITNEY ENGINES FOR B-24 LIBERATOR BOMBERS AND C-47 AND C-53 CARGO PLANES, ALUMINUM AND STEEL FORGINGS, RON AND MAGNESIUM CASTINGS, HIGH-EXPLOSIVE AND ARMOR-PIERCING SHELLS, MILITARY TRUCKS AND MANY OTHER WAR PRODUCTS they had to improvise, borrowing trucks from other units, including the infantry and artillery regiments. However, they also needed drivers, and this is where African American soldiers, who typically served in segregated companies, came to the fore. They would come to form about 75 percent of the Red Ball Express contingent that kept the supplies on the move. Early convoys were often jammed by civilian traffic, but soon, specific routes reserved for the Red Ball truckers were designated, and trucks ideally travelled in convoys of five or more, with a jeep leading the way, as well as one behind for an escort, though smaller groups often were employed. Many Jimmy trucks were overloaded with supplies and many also had their governors disabled so that speeds greater than 55 mph could be attained. Though German airpower was a nuisance, the biggest problem for the Red Ball Express involved continued maintenance, a lack of drivers, and overtired drivers. When it is understood what the Red Ball truckers achieved with such a remarkable vehicle, it is no wonder that General Dwight D. Eisenhower himself deemed the truck one of the most critical weapons of the war. The striking double-page ad featured here well highlights the use of their truck around the world on nearly every continent.

The Jimmy was not the only "deuce and a half" produced during the war. When the Army was accepting bids for their new truck in 1939, Studebaker and International Harvester also submitted designs. While the GMC version was accepted for the U.S. Army, the Studebaker version was also produced beginning in 1941, but all of these vehicles, some 220,000 in all, would go to foreign nations under the Lend-Lease program, the vast majority going to Russia, arriving there from Iran through the Persian Corridor supply route. The Studebaker "deuce and a half" was similar to the GMC, but not as suitable for conditions in Europe and had a shorter operational range. Of the numbers built, about 22,000 were built by REO Motors as a subcontractor beginning in 1944. This cargo truck was very popular with the Russians and was crucial to their war effort, so much so that even Josef Stalin, never one to praise America, sent a personal letter to Studebaker thanking them for the truck. Like the Jimmy, the Studebaker truck was used in many different configurations by the Soviets, some even mounting rocket-launchers. Though the accompanying ad from Studebaker does not mention where most of its trucks were sent, the snowy landscape offers a clue.

Harley-Davidson WLA and Indian 640B, 741, and 841 Motorcycles

The motorcycle as a military weapon had its heyday in World War I, but still had a role to play in World War II. In the former conflict, motorcycle combat units performed front-line service, primarily in the form of armed bikes with sidecars, but during World War II, it soon became evident to Army brass that the versatile jeep would be better suited for many of its former roles. Nonetheless, the military motorcycle had a small but vital role to play, primarily as a fast means of communication, but also as a tool for scouting or reconnaissance work in combat zones, as well as police work on established bases. Interestingly, though Allied motorcycles were not armed with sidecars and used in a strict combat role as German motorcycles were, it was often an American on motorcycle who headed a column of troops or armored vehicles entering a recently liberated city in Europe that gave these motorcycles the popular nickname "Liberators." The Army used several different types of motorcycles during the war, these made by two premier and well-known companies in the history of American bike manufacturing. The most iconic of these bikes was the Harley-Davidson WLA, of which at least 50,000 were built during the war years. This bike had a 45-cubic-inch, 739-cc motor with a three-speed hand shift and had a top speed of 65 mph. In addition to the U.S. Army, thousands of Harley WLAs were also supplied to Russia via Lend-Lease. The WLA was a rugged bike and had a number of interesting features, including an olive-drab or black finish, a crankcase breather which allowed the bike to ford waterways by reducing water intake, black-out head and tail-lights to reduce visibility, and a number of accessories, including a luggage rack for radio gear, an ammunition box, and even a scabbard for a Thompson submachine gun, depicted here in their ad. These bikes would later be used in the Korean War, but were afterwards phased out of service. The Indian Motorcycle Company was based out of Springfield, Massachusetts, and also supplied motorcycles to the army, just as it had in World War I, but could never match their competitor in prestige. Their 640B model was similar to the Harley-Davidson WLA, with the same size motor, while a smaller version, the 741 (often called a "Junior Scout") powered by a 500-cc motor, was also produced. Yet another wartime Indian was the unusual 841 type, which was intended for the desert war in North Africa. This bike was rather unreliable and only about 1,000 were built before the Army abandoned the project, deeming the jeep better suited for those conditions. Overall, Indian produced about 33,000 bikes during the war, but unlike Harley-Davidson, the Indian company would not long survive the war's end, the original company going out of business in 1953. Their ad shown here is interesting, including as a testimony "Ask the Ranger who rides one." Among the Rangers who rode motorcycles during the war was Col. William Darby, who helped form the 1st Ranger Battalion in 1942 and was later killed in action in Italy in 1945, but his bike of choice was the Harley-Davidson, not an Indian. Advertisements for these motorcycle companies did not typically appear in mainstream magazines of the day and as a consequence were usually produced in black and white and in a smaller format such as those shown here.

Landing Vehicle Tracked Alligator (Buffalo)

This unusual amphibious landing/warfare vehicle had its origins in the civilian world, first developed in 1935 by engineer Donald Roebling, the great-grandson of the man who designed the Brooklyn Bridge. Intended as a vehicle suitable for operating in swampy terrain, the Marine Corps became interested in the LVT after seeing an article about Roebling in *Life* magazine. Military prototypes were first developed in 1940, with full-scale production beginning in mid-1941. Overall, nearly 19,000 of these useful vehicles were built, about half of them of the LVT-4 variant. This vehicle was powered by a Continental seven-cylinder radial aircraft engine, was 26 feet long, weighed over 36,000 lb., and could reach a speed of 20 mph on land and 12 knots in the water. The LVT-4 could carry up to twenty-four troops, in addition to its two-man crew, and was a great improvement over prior versions. The armored versions of the LVT-4 were formidable vehicles, carrying a 75-mm howitzer in a turret originally designed for the M8 motor carriage, with some versions even equipped with a Ronson flamethrower. The LVT was used primarily by the U.S. Army and Marine Corp, but also by the British and Australian armies, the British calling their LVTs Buffaloes, while American forces used the vehicle's old civilian name, the Alligator. The LVT was first used at Guadalcanal in a support role and were unarmed, but the Marines that used them soon changed this and made their own modifications to mount machine guns. The LVT first saw combat during the tough fighting at Tarawa, and of the 100 first deployed, only thirty-five remained operational after the first day of fighting. This performance led to changes in design, including

"HERE at (CENSORED) 90% of the motorcycles are Harley-Davidsons and they sure can take a lot of punishment. The territory for miles around is deep sand, steep hills and valleys. A motorcycle has to have a lot to hold up under the treatment we give 'em, and Harley-Davidsons do this with plenty to spare."

That's an example of letters pouring in from all parts of the globe. No wonder thousands of motorcycle enthusiasts are saving up for the day when they can again "twist the throttle" and roll down the highways together. Get lined up for YOUR new Harley-Davidson after the war — BUY WAR BONDS NOW.

Write for free copy of ENTHUSIAST MAGAZINE, filled with illustrated motorcycle stories.

HARLEY-DAVIDSON MOTOR CO.
Dept. F, Milwaukee 1, Wis.

HARLEY-
DAVIDSON
MOTORCYCLES

INDIAN MOTORCYCLES are in warpaint today. We've ripped off the streamlined fenders and hung on a rifle holster; we've discarded for the time being that flashy chrome trim; we've souped up the motor; and hidden those snappy two-toned colors under Army drab.

The vital point is—*they're Indian Motorcycles*... favorites for fighting as for sport. Indian's world-famous power, safety and dependability have already been proved in action on a dozen fighting fronts. *Ask the Ranger who rides one!*

When motorcycles go back to mufti after the war, there'll be new and greater Indians for you to ride. In the meantime, your Indian dealer is the man to help you keep your present machine in good shape . . . and he *may* have a dandy re-conditioned "buy" for you. See him today.

INDIAN MOTOCYCLE COMPANY, SPRINGFIELD, MASS.

BUY WAR BONDS NOW
★ ★ TO BUY AN INDIAN LATER ★ ★

220 *Please mention* POPULAR SCIENCE MONTHLY *whe*

more armor plating, as well as the introduction of a heavily armed LVT-4 to provide fire-support for LVT battalions. Following these changes, the LVT became an indispensable assault vehicle, playing a major role in the Marshall Islands campaign and at Peleliu, where the first LVT flamethrowers were employed. The vehicle probably saw its largest use in the Leyte Gulf landings in October 1944. LVTs were also used in Europe, but on a lesser scale, most notably by the British Army during operations to cross the Rhine River. Interestingly, Donald Roebling was widely applauded for his contribution to the war effort and received the Medal of Merit from President Truman in 1948 for his "outstanding service." The ad here is a typical one for the U.S. Steel Corporation, they usually posing the weapons of war they helped manufacture with everyday items used in peacetime.

M29 Weasel

This curious-looking tracked-vehicle, widely advertised during the war, was built by Studebaker but was conceived in 1942 for a Norwegian military mission that never took place. Nevertheless, this vehicle, which was designed to be air-dropped by parachute and carry enough supplies for a commando team, proved to be useful in many ways and would not see service in truly snowy conditions until after the war had ended. The Weasel was powered by a 70-hp Studebaker six-cylinder engine and could reach the speed of 35 mph over all different kinds of terrain. Manned by a driver and capable of carrying three passengers and about a half-ton of cargo, the M29 had a range of 165 miles and could operate in very shallow water. A variant, the M29C Water Weasel, was built that could operate on rivers, but was not suitable for ocean use. The M29 came off the assembly line unarmed, but in the field a machine gun was often mounted for protection. The M29 was used in many different ways, including as a transport and cargo carrier, a mobile command center, and even as an ambulance, as the vehicle could go where many others could not, including the jeep. In Europe, both American and British forces used the Weasel, including at D-Day, the Battle of the Bulge, and Rhine River operations, while in the Pacific it was used at Iwo Jima and Okinawa, excelling in traversing the volcanic sand and rocky island terrain. Overall, about 16,000 Weasels were built by Studebaker, some of them used later in the Korean War, as well as in peacetime Arctic expeditions. The Weasel's builder advertised heavily during the war the many weapons they helped to build, but no matter which one was being advertised, the B-17 Flying Fortress always makes a cameo appearance.

It's a jungle "Weasel" too!

IN the forbidding tropical undergrowth of the Pacific islands, Studebaker's amazing new Weasel personnel and cargo carrier is now in action with our armed forces.

It's advancing, as it has been doing in Europe, over terrain that seems impossible for any mechanized military vehicle to negotiate.

Swiftly and stealthily, the Weasel glides forward in mud and swamp as well as on sand and snow. And it floats like a boat in lakes and rivers, as its powerful Studebaker Champion engine propels it from shore to shore.

A many-purpose vehicle, this new "Champion" in invasion warfare not only transports men and supplies but also serves to carry wounded back to hospital areas. It's geared to clamber up seemingly impossible grades on its flexible rubber-padded tracks. With its help, light artillery pieces, and the ammunition to feed them, can often be moved up to otherwise inaccessible positions.

Built by Studebaker and powered by the famous Studebaker Champion engine, the Weasel is just one of a number of Studebaker war production assignments which include Wright Cyclone engines for the famous Boeing Flying Fortress as well as heavy-duty Studebaker military trucks.

PIONEER AND PACEMAKER IN AUTOMOTIVE PROGRESS

Now building Wright Cyclone engines for the Boeing Flying Fortress—heavy-duty Studebaker military trucks—the Army's versatile personnel and cargo carrier, the Weasel.

Your War Bonds help keep the Flying Fortresses flying

Keep on buying War Bonds and keep the War Bonds you buy. They're the world's best investment. Every $3 you invest pays you back $4.

Willys MB and Ford GPW Jeep

This legendary vehicle, famed the world over, is by far the best-known weapon deployed by the United States during World War II. Not only were more jeeps, some 648,000 in all, built than any other vehicle by any country during the war, the jeep was also used by every Allied nation. Its numbers and outstanding service were perhaps the epitome of America's industrial strength during the war. Furthermore, the influence of the jeep on the civilian car market after the war was extensive, creating a whole new class of vehicles almost single-handedly and making the term "4×4" a household one in the U.S. and beyond. So much has already been written about the jeep and its origins, so a brief outline of its incredible wartime history will have to suffice here. This quarter-ton command reconnaissance vehicle had its immediate origins in 1939, when the Army decided it needed a standardized light and agile quarter-ton off-road vehicle, as their current inventory of half-ton trucks were just too heavy and slow. In July 1940, the Army sent the formal requirements for the proposed vehicle to over 100 American auto manufacturers, among which three would ultimately respond. The first was the American Bantam Company, followed by Willys Overland, with Ford Motor Company coming in later on. Bantam won the contract and built the first prototype, making it into the Army's hands in September 1940. Willys and Ford would also deliver their prototypes, as it was known that Bantam, a small company with precarious finances, would probably not be able to produce their vehicle in sufficient quantities. In the end, the Army accepted all three companies as manufacturers as testing proceeded and design changes were made. Contrary to popular belief, the design patent was owned by the U.S. government, not Willys, and the jeep really was a collaborative design for which no single company or individual could take full credit. The overall compact size and lines of the jeep came from Bantam's original designs, while the preferred engine was Willy's signature "Go-Devil," a straight-four, 60-hp engine. On the other hand, it was Ford which designed the jeep's signature slotted front grill and gave it the distinctive flat and square hood design. In all, Bantam built only about 2,600 jeeps, and the Army knew it would need many more, so turned to Willys, who built just over 360,000 of them, and Ford, who built about 280,000 jeeps, including over 50,000 exported to Russia under Lend-Lease. As to the name "jeep," the exact origin for the term as it applies to this particular vehicle has been hotly-debated and much written about. The term "jeep" itself was used as far back as World War I as slang for new troops and also was applied to any new or experimental vehicle. There was also a 1930s cartoon character, which went by the name "jeep," while some believe that the term was derived from the Army's designation of the car as a general-purpose (GP) vehicle. No matter who coined the term, it was the Willys company that popularized it during their great publicity events surrounding the new vehicle, which included driving one up the steps of the Capitol Building in Washington, D.C., during a 1941 press event. Beginning in 1942, the jeep was supplied to every Army unit, with about 150 of them going to each infantry unit, and by 1944 there were so many jeeps on the road during the Allied drive on Germany that enemy troops almost believed that every soldier was issued his own jeep. Whether loaded with supplies, troops, or a combination of both, often armed with a machine gun, the jeep was a workhorse, solid and dependable, and was a beloved vehicle by the soldiers who drove them, it being the closest any American would ever come to driving a sporty car. After the war, with Willys Overland gaining the trademark after the demise of Bantam, the Jeep CJ (Civilian Jeep) 4×4 was the pioneer sport-utility vehicle (SUV), a historical milestone in American automotive history. Despite the fact that Ford's contribution to the jeep, both in terms of design and numbers produced was significant, it seems to have ceded the battle to Willys in the civilian market and its role in bringing the jeep to life has largely been forgotten by all but military historians and today's jeep enthusiasts. As with several other weapons mentioned above, the jeep's usefulness was such that it was credited as being one of the top machines that helped the Allies win the war. It is for this reason, combined with its innovative design, that the jeep was also designated in 1991 as a Historic Mechanical Engineering Landmark by the American Society of Mechanical Engineers. As mentioned previously, Willys-Overland advertised their jeep heavily during the war, commissioning a series of ads, perhaps the finest of the war in artistic terms, which shows it in operation in a number of different theatres. Ford ads for their jeep, however, are comparatively few in number and were usually printed in black and white.

THE SATURDAY EVENING POST

• • To millions of people all over the world "JEEP" means WILLYS • •

The Sun Never Sets on the Mighty "Jeep"

BASTOGNE OR DIE

TRUSTY "JEEP" DELIVERS THE GENERAL

On the 29th of December last, newspapers were ablaze with the story of an American paratroop general's hair-raising trip to get to his heroic men cut off by the Nazis at Bastogne in the "Belgian Bulge".

By special plane he was flown from Washington across the Atlantic to the Western Front. There, in a tough, little battle-scarred "Jeep" he and two companions raced across the country, hell-bent for Bastogne and his beleaguered men.

Over rough, wintry forest trails . . . dodging fallen trees . . . crashing over frozen ruts . . . streaking past pop-eyed German patrols . . . feeling the hot breath of death-baited bullets . . . now crawling . . . now climbing . . . now twisting . . . now crouching motionless . . . the plucky "Jeep" fought its perilous way through the Nazi lines.

Failure of any part of the "Jeep" would have meant "curtains" for the mission. But it *didn't fail!* "Jeep" performance, "Jeep" dependability and "Jeep" ruggedness *came through again.* The general was delivered to his courageous men—and another "mission completed" was added to the already glorious record of the mighty "Jeep".

★ ★ ★

We have received many letters asking us about postwar "Jeeps." Among the numerous "Jeep" uses suggested in this postwar planning are, operating farm implements, towing, trucking, road work, operating power devices and many personal business and pleasure uses. Does the "Jeep" figure in *your* postwar plans? Willys-Overland Motors, Inc., Toledo 1, Ohio.

The Sun Never Sets On the Mighty "Jeep".

VIVE LES AMERICAINS! VIVE LA FRANCE! VIVE LE JEEP!

A WORD PICTURE OF THE HOUR OF LIBERATION IN ORLEANS, 1944

IN THE morning of August 17th, 1944, Nazi-infested Orleans came suddenly alive. The [illegible] was charged with suppressed excitement. Emo[illegible]ns were masked, but French hearts beat wildly. [illegible] the glorious news was being flashed from lip to ear, that the victorious Americans were marching toward the city. Liberation was at hand.

All that day and night the air trembled from the violence of the fighting. Next morning a joyful, almost hysterical Orleans realized that the hated Nazis had fled.

Soon the welcome roar of American motors was heard, and the people streamed forth from their homes and shops.

Some hastened toward the oncoming Americans. Others gathered round the statue of Joan of Arc.

Into the city and straight to the square the first Americans came—strong, forthright young fighting men with friendly grins on their battle-stained faces. For a few seconds the deep emotions of the people held their lips silent. Then a single clarion voice pierced the stillness—"Vive le Jeep," it crie[illegible] And the crowd, their suppressed emotions su[illegible]denly released, shouted, cried, wept and join[illegible] the chorus—"Vive Les Americains! Vive la Franc[illegible] *Vive le Jeep."*

> *In the center of the city square in Orleans, looking out over the gleaming river Loire, there stands a statue of Joan of Arc, the saint-like peasant maiden who in 1429, led an awed and inspired army against the enemies of France, raised the critical siege of Orleans, and saved France for Frenchmen. Today her name is hallowed throughout all of France as a saint and the immortal liberator.*

And so, in the shadow of the statue of th[illegible] saintly liberator, Joan of Arc, the overjoyed peop[illegible] of Orleans gave thanks to a modern deliver[illegible] who came, not on a prancing white horse, but [illegible] steeds of steel called "Jeeps."

★ ★ ★

In France and in every country in the world, [illegible] mighty "Jeep" is a symbol of freedom and [illegible] American genius—clean, rugged, tough and [illegible]pendable! A mighty servant in war—and a mig[illegible] servant for the coming dawn of a golden era [illegible] peace. Willys-Overland Motors, Inc., Toledo 1, Oh[illegible]

Willys *Builds the Mighty* **'Jeep'**

Sweethearts
FORD MASS-PRODUCTION LINES DELIVER FLEETS OF WEAPONS
JEEPS • AMPHIBIAN JEEPS • M-4 TANKS • M-10 TANK DESTROYERS • PRATT & WHITNEY AIRCRAFT ENGINES • ARMY TRUCKS
CONSOLIDATED LIBERATOR BOMBERS • TRANSPORT GLIDERS • UNIVERSAL CARRIERS • TANK ENGINES • TRUCK AND JEEP ENGINES
ARMOR PLATE • GUN MOUNTS • AIRCRAFT GENERATORS • TURBO-SUPERCHARGERS • RATE-OF-CLIMB INDICATORS • MAGNESIUM CASTINGS
This list does not include other important Victory models now in production that cannot be named due to wartime conditions.
FULL PRODUCTION FOR VICTORY

of the A.E.F.!

"Roughriders" of America's Armed Forces Admire the Tough, Sure-Footed, Ford-Made Jeeps and Amphibian Jeeps—Built to Charge Roughshod Through the Toughest Going Any Army Ever Faced!

JUST as a trooper loves his horse and a sailor his ship, America's fighting men in this mechanized war have come to think the world and all of the rough-and-ready, game little Jeeps! Mass-produced on the same lines that turned out automobiles, Ford has made thousands of both land Jeeps and Amphibian Jeeps, each built with the traditional precision and cost-saving skill acquired in producing more than 30,000,000 Ford cars and trucks.

They're sweethearts, say the soldiers! And it's no wonder they're hailed with affection by our armed forces everywhere in this global conflict! Fast, durable and mule-footed, Ford-made Jeeps are ruggedly built, and have the stout-hearted capacity to smash through to their objective no matter how tough the going.

They charge roughshod through thickets and jungles that would trap a less formidable vehicle. With their four-wheel drive, they nimbly scale slippery banks and steep hillsides, "turn on a dime," do fifty over corduroy roads and shell-pocked terrain—and do it all with a minimum of care and attention!

Together with such other battle-tried products as M-4 tanks and M-10 tank destroyers, Liberator bombers and heavy horsepower aircraft engines, these Jeeps give practical expression to the Ford wartime creed of *full production for Victory!*

FORD MOTOR COMPANY

AMPHIBIAN JEEP

The Ford-Developed Amphibian Jeep is equally at home on water or land—can cross swift rivers, lakes and even traverse open seas for limited distances. If necessary the Amphibian Jeep can pull itself up a well-nigh sheer bank by means of a power capstan in the prow. The same steering controls are used without change for land or water operation and most parts are interchangeable with the quarter-ton Ford truck.

7

Guns and Other Ordnance

The ads for this category of weapons, especially those for personal or handheld firearms, are both interesting and very distinctly highlight American traditions surrounding the sport of hunting. Indeed, in many cases, the act of fighting the Axis enemy with these weapons was often advertised by such companies as Western Ammunition, Remington, and Winchester as being akin to the peacetime sport of hunting, with images of the enemy juxtaposed with that of duck and game hunters. Of course, many of these same companies also advertised the fact that, when the war was won, their products would once again be available to the hunting public so that that great American sport could resume. Not surprisingly, many of these ads, especially those by traditional firearms companies, appeared in hunting-related magazines such as *Field & Stream*. Author Thomas L. Altherr details these ads and describes how they were used to bolster the image of a sport that had been declining in prestige before the war, and whose proponents hoped that in the aftermath of the war, a revival might be sparked. The ad shown here is an excellent example of this hunting ideal. As Altherr contends, many of these company's advertisements promoted the idea held by the hunting community that hunters at home made for better soldiers abroad. As might be expected, the larger the weapon advertised, the farther away it gets, in general, from the theme of game or wildfowl hunting, usually due to the fact that companies like Pontiac, manufacturer of larger weapons like the Oerlikon and Bofors guns, had no relation to the hunting industry whatsoever.

M1911 Pistol and M1917 Revolver Sidearms

These sidearms were widely produced during the war and were based on models first developed around the time of World War I, each also available in civilian models. The M1911, also known as the "Colt Government" was first developed in 1911 by Colt, being a single-shot semi-automatic .45-cal. pistol. A version of this iconic sidearm is still used by the Marine Corps today. Hundreds of thousands of these pistols were manufactured by Colt, Remington, the Ithaca Gun Company, and even a small amount by the Singer Sewing Machine Company during the war, and it was used by nearly all Allied forces as the preferred sidearm, especially by commando or special force units, but was also standard issue for American officers. The M1917 Revolver, as its numerical designation suggests, was first supplied to the military in 1917 and was produced by Colt and Smith & Wesson. This six-shot, large frame revolver is also a classic firearm that seemed to be a favorite among tank and artillery crews, but was also supplied to Britain's Royal Navy during the war. This Colt ad is notable for its distinct post-war emphasis.

M1 Garand Rifle

This .30-06-cal. semi-automatic rifle was first used by the U.S. Army beginning in 1936, being the first standard issue of this type of rifle. It was named after its designer, John Garand, who worked at the U.S. Army's Springfield Armory, and after many trials and

Millions of 'Small Arms' Essential to Victory
The sporting arms industry of America, long skilled in the ways of gun-making, undertook a tremendous task in production of arms for our Government and its Allies.
The record of its achievement, in quality and stupendous quantity . . . is a vital factor in America's guarantee of victory.
"Savage" with its thousands of workers is proud to be a part of this industry's important war effort. Reports from all parts of the globe record the effective performance of the Browning Aircraft Machine Guns, and other guns and military rifles produced in our plants.
SAVAGE ARMS CORPORATION · UTICA, N.Y.
SAVAGE
ARMY E NAVY
Since award to Savage of the Army-Navy "E", new and higher production schedules have been exceeded.
Savage Automatic Shotguns
Will resume their steady rise in popularity which . . . before the war . . . culminated in the introduction of the lightweight model for upland hunting.

JULY • 1944
63
There's a Great Day Comin'!
FORGET OLD TROUBLES HERE
The pleasant, peaceful shots that will some day ring out from Colt Revolvers and Automatic Pistols in the great outdoors will be a salute to you hardware men and sporting goods dealers! Your patriotism and patience deserve it. That's why Colt's 1944 advertising pictures the "great days comin'" when sportsmen will seek the recreation well-earned by all good Americans. Your store again will be that "Port o' Sport" from which they'll set out with duds, tackle, and better-than-ever Colt's. We share your anticipation and will be ready, when restrictions are lifted, to supply you with those proved leaders in target and outdoor shooting. Shown here are three Colt models that you'll recall with pleasure and can re-stock with profit . . . when Victory has been won.
COLT
Colt Super .38 Automatic Pistol
– Caliber .38 Automatic. A favorite for All Around Service.
Colt Officer's Model Revolver
– Caliber .22 Long Rifle. Leader among .22 caliber revolvers for target shooting.
Colt Target Woodsman
– Caliber .22 Long Rifle. Tops for outdoor service.
COLT'S PATENT FIRE ARMS MFG. CO., HARTFORD, CONNECTICUT

reworkings, finally entered service in 1940 to replace the bolt-action M1903 Springfield rifle. The Army was fully equipped with the M1 by December 1941, just in time, and some 5.4 million were manufactured during the war by several different companies. The average cost of the Garand was about $85 and they were used by every branch of the U.S. military and were regarded as an excellent weapon, being the most modern rifle of its type available. Weighing in at a hefty 10 pounds, the rifle's bulky form made it a bit difficult to carry, but the M1 more than made up for this deficiency in its ability to operate efficiently in the most brutal conditions. The M1 first saw action in the Pacific, and had its first baptism by fire in the fight against the Germans in North Africa. Gaining high praise from men like General George Patton, and the weapon used by numerous Medal of Honor recipients, the M1 Garand was truly a war-winning weapon. The Garand continued in use through the Korean War and even into the Vietnam War, and once phased out of service, became a popular gun for civilian target shooting and hunting, and remains so to this day. This ad from main ammunition and rifle supplier Western notes that its weapons "are hastening the doom of the Axis," and also pays homage to the veterans of its home-state of Illinois in subdued fashion.

M1 Carbine

This light-weight .30-cal. semi-automatic carbine rifle was developed as an alternative to the M1 Garand. Though the idea of developing a lighter gun than the Garand was first proposed in 1938, it was not until 1940 when the requirements were approved, and in 1941 American manufacturers began to submit their proposals. Despite its similar designation to the M1 Garand and similar look, the two weapons were actually completely different, the carbine using a different ammunition altogether and being half the weight of the Garand. It was primarily designed for infantry support troops to carry, such as radiomen, mortarmen, and even combat medics and paratroopers, who also had additional equipment to carry as part of their support roles. Because of its widespread use by a variety of troops, over six million M1 carbines were manufactured during the war, more than any other American gun. Though the weapon was designed by Winchester, it was manufactured in huge numbers by nine large companies, including IBM (about 347,000), the juke-box and pin-ball company Rock-Ola (229,000), Underwood Typewriter (546,000), as well as Winchester (828,000), and the largest producer of them all, the Inland Division of General Motors (over 2.6 million). The performance of the M1 carbine was considered excellent when used in the support role for which it was intended, but when used by front-line troops was considered to not have enough fire-power, especially amongst airborne units. The M1 was largely replaced by the Army with the M2 carbine, but some soldiers were still equipped with the M1 even during the Vietnam War. This interesting ad from Underwood states their traditional role as "Former and future makers of typewriters."

M1903A4 Springfield Sniper Rifle

This weapon was the U.S. Army's primary sniper rifle used in World War II, one that was a derivative of the M1903 Springfield .30-06 bolt-action rifle. That rifle was the Army's primary infantry rifle from its inception in 1903 until it was replaced by the M1 Garand at the beginning of the war. Because there were not enough Garands to go around at first, the Springfield was still used by some units. However, it was the sniper rifle version that saw the most use. This rifle had a range of about 600 yards and was used from about 1943 to the end of the war. The sniper rifle used Redfield scope mounts and the Weaver scope, their advertisement shown here, which had many flaws, including low-power magnification, a lack of waterproofing which made the scope fog up at times, and a poor field of view. Eventually, those M1903A4s used by the Marines switched to another, more powerful scope by the end of the war. Deliveries of this sniper rifle ceased in early 1944, and by 1949, the long-serving Springfield rifle in all its variations was generally phased out of service, though the weapon still saw limited use as late as the Vietnam War.

Browning M1919A4 Machine Gun and M2 AN Aircraft Machine Gun

The .30-cal. M1919A4 medium machine gun was one of the most versatile weapons ever produced for the American military, used in all theatres during World War II. The M1919 employed a five-man crew, which included the squad leader, gunner, assistant gunner, and two ammunition carriers. Mounted on a light-weight and low-profile tripod, the M1919 weighed 31

Our Boys are Better Protected... and Carry More Punch than We Did

2 Reasons Why U. S. Casualties Will Be Held to the Minimum

EVERY American soldier who carries the fast-firing Winchester Carbine is practically a one-man machine gun nest.

Thousands formerly armed with the service pistol are now equipped with this light, hard-hitting weapon developed by Western's Winchester division. As modern as our army itself, it increases the offensive fire-power of an infantry division by practically *one-third*.

With the Winchester Carbine and the famous Garand rifle that enables our troops to plug the enemy with 8 shots while he's returning less than 4, our boys are better protected and they can really "turn on the heat".

Here's American foresight and ingenuity at its best, helping to hold our casualty lists to the very minimum—*First:* because the U. S. Ordnance Department saw that today's small arms must provide more effective screens of offensive and protective firepower, and *Second:* because industry and individuals had the skill and experience to produce such remarkable improvements in arms.

Western's Winchester division is manufacturing both of these remarkable weapons in quantities that are hastening the doom of the Axis.

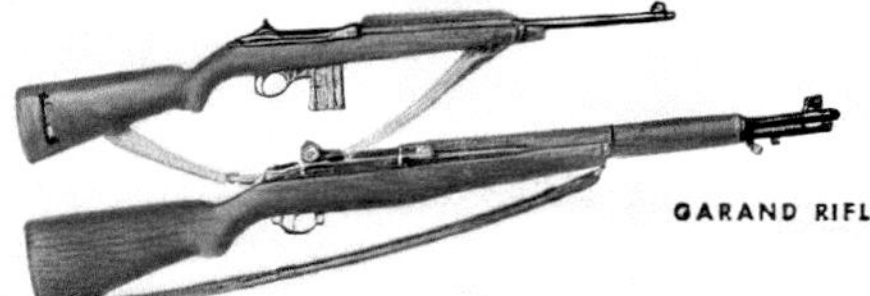

CARBINE PROVIDES SCREEN OF FIRE 6 TIMES DEEPER

Four out of 5 of our troops formerly armed with service pistols are being equipped with the Winchester semi-automatic carbine, U. S. Carbine, Caliber .30 M1. This battle-proved, ultra-modern weapon delivers 15 aimed shots effective at 300 yards, as fast as the trigger can be squeezed. That means fire-power of nearly *double the intensity and 6 times greater range!* The carbine was developed by Winchester in less time than any military small arm on record.

FAST-FIRING GARAND DEADLY AT MORE THAN ½ MILE

Amazing stories about individual exploits with the famous Garand semi-automatic rifle have come from battlefront correspondents and the men themselves. Typical is that of an American sergeant in Sicily who accounted for 8 charging Germans with the 8 shots in his cartridge clip. Western's Winchester division, long in quantity production of Garands, was able to *cut their cost to less than ½ the original contract price.*

AN AVALANCHE OF AMMUNITION

From Western-operated plants at East Alton, Ill., New Haven, Conn., and the St. Louis Ordnance Plant, operated by The United States Cartridge Company, a Western subsidiary, we have already supplied the armed forces with more than 5 billion .30 and .50 caliber rifle and machine gun cartridges.

CARTRIDGES BY THE BILLIONS...

FOR EVERY FRONT

CARTRIDGE COMPANY
EAST ALTON, ILL.

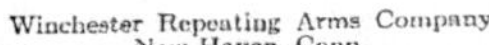
Winchester Repeating Arms Company, New Haven, Conn. | The United States Cartridge Company, St. Louis, Missouri | Bond Electric Corporation, New Haven, Conn. | Olin Corporation (Aluminum Division), Tacoma, Wash. | And Other Divisions and Affiliates

Note the CARBINE...
"...increases fire power 33%!"
"After 35 years, the Army goes from the pistol to the carbine . . . The Winchester carbine is rated high, and is judged to increase the fire power of the infantry regiment by 33 per cent."
As reported by a prominent news magazine
"All the men and officers in the infantry who have been armed with the pistol will carry the carbine instead . . . It fires a .30 calibre cartridge and is accurate up to any distance that soldiers usually fire at the enemy . . . We believe it to be a weapon of great merit . . ."
Robert P. Patterson, Under Secretary of War
The same manufacturing ability that has made Underwood Elliott Fisher typewriters, adding and accounting machines famous throughout the world, is now being applied to the production of carbines.
TO OUR MILLIONS OF VALUED CUSTOMERS: TYPEWRITERS—New and used typewriters are sold only to the U. S. Government for the armed services. You may rent used machines under Office of Price Administration regulations.
ADDING AND ACCOUNTING MACHINES—New machines are available under War Production Board regulations. We have been able to assist many of our customers with their accounting problems.
RIBBONS, CARBON PAPER, ETC.—We may sell ribbons, carbon paper and other supplies for all types of office machines without restriction.
MAINTENANCE—Our maintenance service is in complete and efficient operation from coast to coast to help you keep your Underwood, Elliott Fisher and Sundstrand machines operating efficiently and we are permitted to manufacture necessary parts.
Carbines are now in mass production by
Underwood Elliott Fisher Company
Former and future makers of Typewriters, Adding and Accounting Machines
★Enlist Your Dollars Buy More War Bonds To Shorten The Duration

AMERICA'S JUNGLE TROOPS TAKE OFF!
• Wherever there's a job to be done, you'll find these eager young Americans going into battle—on foot, in half-tracks, jeeps, or giant transport planes. Every man knows his business, and has the equipment he needs to defeat the enemy. American snipers, for example, have the advantage of the Weaver Model 330 Scope for their rifles—and it's no wonder they spread sudden death wherever they get a long shot at the enemy. It's a mighty good scope—the same scope you liked so well in hunting.
WEAVER
Scopes and Chokes
MADE IN EL PASO, TEXAS BY W R. WEAVER CO.
YOUR DEALER has the Weaver-Choke, price $9.75 with any two choke tubes. If he doesn't have it in stock, write us. He probably has some Weaver Scopes also; if not, write us. We may be able to help you.

pounds, though fixed mounts for the Browning were also carried on many vehicles, including jeeps, tanks, half-tracks, amphibious vehicles, and almost any other vehicle you could name. This machine gun could fire up to 600 rounds per minute and had a maximum range of 1,500 yards. The gun was air-cooled, a vast improvement over its predecessor, the water-cooled M1917 machine gun. Nearly 440,000 were produced during the war. One important outgrowth of this gun was the M2 AN (Army-Navy) aircraft machine gun. Mounted as either fixed or moveable guns on the many fighters, bombers, and patrol planes flown by the U.S. military during the war, as well as some Allied aircraft, this version of the Browning weighed about two-thirds that of the M1919 and had a faster rate of fire, up to 1,200 rounds per minute. One interesting aspect of the M2 was its auto-feed belt mechanism, which was well engineered but very complex, making the aircraft-mounted Brownings one of the most difficult weapons to repair in the field. The maker of the ammunition belts that fed the Browning machine gun, the Hughes Aircraft Company, was started by the famed and flamboyant Howard Hughes, whose plant before the war employed but a handful of full-time employees, but grew to 80,000 by the end of the war. Howard Hughes gained further renown after the war for building the prototype of a huge, eight-engine flying boat nicknamed *The Spruce Goose*, in 1947, and in the later years of his life was known for being an eccentric recluse.

Browning Automatic Rifle (BAR) M1918

This interesting light machine gun was first developed in 1918, too late to see significant service in World War I, and only became standard issue in 1938. The BAR, as this weapon came to be known, fired a .30-06 Springfield cartridge and could fire up to 650 rounds per minute, with a range of about 4,500 yards. The BAR was the only fire support weapon in a twelve-man squad, first operated by a three-man team which included a gunner, assistant gunner, and ammunition carrier, though all men in the squad were trained in its use. Later, BAR teams were reduced to two and, later, one-man teams. The BAR was designed to provide tactical support to primary infantry troops, but very soon the BAR was found to have a slower rate of fire than automatic weapons employed by German troops, so two BAR teams were eventually supplied to a squad to make up for this deficiency. While the BAR could be fired from the hip, it is also recognized for the bi-pod mount it often used. Though the BAR saw extensive use during the war, including even being standard issue to Navy submarine crews, it was a weapon plagued by a small magazine capacity (twenty rounds), and production issues and the supply never met the demand. The BAR remained in use into the Vietnam War era, though it was obsolete by then, but was still used by Army National Guard units in the 1970s, even though production ceased in 1945. This testimonial-style ad for the Harvel Watch Company highlights the BAR and its use by Edson's Raiders, describing the rapid-fire recoil that made it "a shaking fool."

M1 and M3 Sub-Machine Guns

The U.S. military used two types of submachine guns during World War II, the "Tommy" gun and the "Greaser." The M1 Thompson submachine gun, known as the "Tommy" gun, is a classic weapon that was well-known by the public in 1930s and 1940s America. It was developed in 1918 by John Thompson and is famed for its distinctive silhouette, which includes a vertical foregrip and the round drum magazine. The gun, which fires a .45-cal. cartridge, could fire up to 800 rounds per minute. This gun was sold on the civilian market, though it was expensive, and became the weapon of choice of gangsters in the Prohibition Era, especially in Chicago, where it had many nicknames, including the "Chicago Piano," or "The Chopper." Other groups that used the gun include the FBI, the U.S. Postal Service (in limited quantities), the Marine Corps, and even the Irish Republican Army. In 1938, the U.S. Army adopted the Thompson as its submachine gun of choice, and during the war over 1.5 million were manufactured, many by Savage Arms. The M1 version used during the war utilized a thirty-round ammunition box instead of the classic drum magazine used by earlier models. The gun was used by scouts, raiders, Rangers, paratroopers, tank crews, and commando units of both the British and American armies, as well as the Canadians. It was a popular gun to use, and very effective at close range in the war in Europe, but was not well suited for the tropical war in the Pacific where it was less effective due to jungle conditions. Despite the fact that the M3 submachine gun was developed as a replacement mid-war, the "Tommy" gun remained the most important weapon in this category and deliveries kept coming into 1944. The M3 was developed beginning in late 1942 after the Army saw how effective the German submachine gun and the British Sten gun were in comparison to the Thompson. General Motors was given the task of designing the new weapon, to be made of all sheet-metal, capable of firing 450 rounds per minute and with a range of about 100 yards. It was meant to be a cheap and disposable gun, once it malfunctioned it would be discarded for another. It was nicknamed the "Greaser" for its resemblance to a mechanic's grease gun, and went into production beginning in 1943. Though some 607,000 were produced during the war, early on problems with the gun were encountered which resulted in several design improvements and the gun was never as popular as the Thompson. The ad featured here showing a soldier with a Thompson from Burroughs, known for their adding machines (the forerunner of the calculator), made Norden bombsights during the war but not, as far as is known, the Thompson gun.

M1 Anti-Tank Rocket Launcher (Bazooka)

This distinctive tube-shaped weapon is important as a first-generation example of a rocket-propelled anti-tank weapon. Rifle grenade launchers had previously been developed for the Army's infantry weapons, like the Garand and Springfield, but these were not effective

Here is an excerpt from an actual letter received from a United States Marine:

"I was in Edson's Raiders, U.S.M.C., the first to land on Tulagi. For over a year I battered my Harvel Watch in rugged training and rougher combat. My weapon was a Browning automatic rifle, a light, shoulder-fired machine gun—a shaking fool.

"The shattering vibration of firing the gun had no more effect on the mechanical operation of my Harvel watch than the landings in sea water. My watch was never off more than a minute or two in a month's time.

"I have often had occasion to bless my wife for sending me this silent watch. In a listening post in the jungle, when your very breathing and heartbeat are audible a couple of feet away, a noisy ticker on a Nip's wrist has sent plenty of Sons of Heaven to join their ancestors. The only way I can tell if my Harvel is running is to look at the sweep second hand."

With each day of the war, evidence of Harvel dependability grows and grows. On land, on sea and in the sky, the sturdy Harvel watch is winning new honors in every branch of the service.

HARVEL

One of America's Fine Watches

HARVEL WATCH COMPANY • ROCKEFELLER CENTER, NEW YORK, 20

against tanks. By 1942, the Army had a grenade-shaped charge capable of stopping a tank, but needed a way to deliver it, finding it in a simple tube that weighed less than thirteen pounds and was 55 inches long. Thus, the "Bazooka" was born and entered service in late 1942. The weapon gained its unusual nickname due to its resemblance to a strange tubular musical instrument invented by radio comedian Bob Burns, which he called a "bazooka." American forces first used the bazooka in North Africa, though many legends recount the fact that the day before they were first used in battle, no troops had actually received training on how to use it. Perhaps because of this, the introduction of the bazooka was a disaster; it proved unreliable and played no role in fighting the Germans, with no enemy tank known to have even been hit. Further, the Germans captured some bazookas and went on to develop their own type which was very superior to the bazooka. Though the bazooka was plagued with problems and proved ineffective at knocking out German tanks, it was useful in disabling tanks at a close-range by hitting their treads, as well as destroying enemy emplacements and fortifications. Despite its mixed performance, the bazooka was an effective weapon in many cases, and while not a game-changer, it did mark a new era in modern warfare. Interestingly, the bazooka was heavily sold to the American public, often advertised as packing the punch of a 155-mm howitzer, which was a wild exaggeration, though this ad from U.S. Steel merely touts its steel composition.

M1 and M2 Portable Flamethrowers

This fearsome weapon was first developed by the Army in 1940 and went into service in 1942. The unit was configured like a backpack, the first version, the M1, weighing 72 lb., with a fuel capacity of 5 gallons and a range of about 50 feet. The improved M2, which entered service in 1943, weighed 65 lb. and had a much greater range of nearly 150 feet, though its burn rate was only seven seconds. Both units had a battery pack to generate a spark which ignited the hydrogen carried in one tank, which in turn ignited the napalm (thickened fuel) carried in another tank, the flame shooting out of a hand-held long, thin pipe.

The first use of the flamethrower against Japanese fortifications in late 1942 was a failure, leading to the improved M2. The flamethrowers proved deadly effective in clearing out enemy fortifications and pillboxes in both theatres of the war, though close-fire support was needed due to their limited range. The M2 and its variants were employed in the Korean and Vietnam Wars, though was phased out before the end of the later conflict. This ad from Nash-Kelvinator was one in a series of ads which got into the mindset of a soldier.

M2 Mortar

Several different types of mortar weapons were used by U.S. forces during the war. The M2 was developed in the late 1930s as a more portable version of the heavier, 81-mm M1 mortar, both of which were based on the design of a French engineer. The M2 went into production early in 1940 and was intended as a light infantry support weapon, firing a 60-mm 3-lb. shell, and with a range of just over a mile. The M2 weighed about 42 lb. and was manned by three men, including a gunner, loader, and ammunition carrier, with mortar squad units usually part of a weapons platoon This very popular and high-performing weapon was used in both an offensive and defensive role, providing indirect fire support and were invaluable in attacking troops that were entrenched in ground fortifications, with mortar crews able to lob up to eighteen shells a minute. Approximately 60,000 M2s were manufactured during the war, and it remained in the U.S. arsenal into the 1970s. The ad for this weapon comes from a company better known for the railroad cars it produced in peacetime.

MKIIA1 Fragmentation Hand Grenade

This well-known weapon, often called the "pineapple" due to its textured shape, was first manufactured in 1918 and was a standard weapon in the U.S. Army, with the MKIIA1 appearing in 1942. This hand grenade was made of cast iron and filled with 2 ounces of TNT,

which was detonated after the ring-held safety pin was pulled. It was equipped with a five-second time fuse delay, which gave a soldier time to lob it at its target. Once it exploded, the iron case of the grenade would shatter, creating fragments that flew in every direction and caused destruction within a short radius. While estimates vary, it is thought that up to 50 million grenades of this variety were manufactured during the war. This interesting ad from General Electric features not only their X-ray technology used in testing grenade fuses, but also mentions their famed radio programs, including the GE all-girl orchestra.

Howitzer Field Artillery (75-mm, 105-mm, 155-mm, 240-mm)

The howitzer was the U.S. Army's main artillery piece during the war, such guns manufactured in varying sizes depending on their intended use. This type of artillery piece overall is distinguished by its short barrel and the use of a propellant to launch their shells at a high trajectory over a long distance. The weapon was a ubiquitous one during World War II, with many 75-mm pack howitzers mounted on gun carriages being on display at VFW and American Legion posts around the country, as well as in many town parks and other public spaces. The 75-mm pack howitzer (so-called because it was first pulled by pack mules) was developed in the 1920s, but due to a lack of funds, less than a hundred were in Army units by 1940. Mass production began in 1941, and by the end of the war some 5,000 had been manufactured. This small version of the howitzer was used by field artillery regiments, but also airborne troops, while the 10th Mountain Division had three battalions of the weapon. The 105-mm howitzer was manufactured beginning in 1941 and was considered an excellent weapon, capable of lobbing a high-explosive shell over 12,000 yards in an infantry support role. In general, each Army artillery regiment had three battalions of the 105-mm, each equipped with twelve guns and operated in batteries of four guns. Over 8,500 of this variant were manufactured during the war. The 155-mm howitzer was also built beginning in 1942 and was deployed in the same fashion as the 105-mm. The largest and most powerful artillery gun produced by the U.S. during the war was the 240-mm "Black Dragon" howitzer. It was able to fire a 360-lb. shell over 25,000 yards and was designed to penetrate heavy concrete fortifications. It was designed in 1942 and first saw service at Anzio in January 1944, and was later used in the Italian campaign at Monte Cassino, destroying the famous monastery there. The gun was also used in the Pacific during the Battle of Manilla, but since heavily fortified targets were few, it did not see wide use. A total 315 units of this monster, manned by fourteen men, were built during the war. All of the howitzers except the 240-mm were also extensively used by Allied armies, many acquired via Lend-Lease. Though this GM Truck and Coach ad depicts a 105-mm howitzer and gun carriage, it focuses more on the GMC trucks that were made to get this gun to where it was needed.

Oerlikon 20-mm Naval Antiaircraft Cannon

This famed cannon, first produced in 1937, was actually based on a German design from the 1920s. Because Oerlikon was based in neutral Switzerland, they sold their products to any and all countries, the 20-mm cannon used to arm fighter aircraft, including the German Bf 109, as well as naval vessels and shore-based anti-aircraft batteries. From 1942 onwards, the U.S. Navy made it their anti-aircraft gun of choice, it being manufactured in the U.S. under license from Oerlikon during the war. Ammunition was fed into this cannon via a sixty-round drum magazine, though belt-fed versions were also developed. In the Navy, the Oerlikon was typically used in a twin-mount, or quadruple-mount format for extra firepower, with the latter even mounted on a few PT boats operating in the Mediterranean. This cannon was a one-man weapon, held in place by a waist-belt and shoulder support, with some mountings being height adjustable based on the size of the gunner. Sighting was achieved with a simple ring and bead sight. All of the 20-mm Oerlikons built in the U.S. were manufactured by the Pontiac Division of General Motors, they making some 5,700 in all, as depicted in this ad.

Bofors 40-mm Anti-Aircraft Cannon

This cannon was produced under license from the Swedish arms company Bofors. It was first designed in 1930 and went into production beginning in 1932. This gun actually posed manufacturing problems for American companies, as production documents had to be translated from Swedish, and measurements converted from metric, but production was underway

THE SATURDAY EVENING POST

IT MUSTN'T bite the hand that throws it

HIS IS A HAND GRENADE. When you pull firing pin and release the lever you have the length of time it takes the fuse to burn n to get rid of it or get away from there— that's only a handful of seconds!

f you made hand grenades, or used them, 'd want to be mighty sure about those fuses. You can be. The fuse of this grenade, and usands of others just like it, was individ- ly X-rayed while passing down a produc- n line at the rate of 4000 an hour. When a d fuse showed up, something equivalent to the signal for a four-alarm fire took place. A bell rang, a red light flashed, the bad fuse was automatically daubed with red paint, and finally, to make assurance doubly sure that the bad fuse didn't slip through, it was recorded on the chart of a photoelectric meter.

From sorting oranges for California fruit growers to sorting hand grenades is quite a step—but it is typical of the new wartime jobs G-E scientists and engineers have put X rays to work on. It is also typical of the application of G.E.'s peacetime research and engineering to war.

Nearly twenty years ago Dr. William D. Coolidge, now G-E vice-president and Director of the Research Laboratory, developed the Coolidge X-ray tube—one of the most important developments of all time in science and medicine. In the years that followed, he and other scientists and engineers worked steadily to improve this almost magical tool of research and healing.

Then came the war, and the X ray in its latest and most powerful form became almost overnight a vital tool of war production, testing for hidden flaws no human eyes could reveal the metals on which the strength and endurance of our arms depend.

Which makes the X ray another good example of the way G-E research and engineering work to meet America's needs—constantly, in unexpected ways—in war and peace. *General Electric Company, Schenectady, N. Y.*

The G-E million-volt X ray cuts from hours to minutes the time required to examine metal parts—from airplane crankshafts to turbine shells.

Hear the General Electric radio programs: "The G-E All-girl Orchestra" Sunday 10 p.m. EWT, NBC—"The World Today" news, every weekday 6:45 p.m. EWT, CBS.

GMC transport trucks carry troops across a new type rubber pontoon bridge during night maneuvers. In actual combat, black-out lights would be used. ACME PHOTO

Warmly clothed against Iceland's cold, U. S. Artillery unit holds target practice with 105 mm. howitzer. GMC truck pulls gun, carries crew and ammunition. ACME PHOTO

Around the clock, all around the world, GMC military vehicles are helping to turn the tide against the Axis. Whenever truck power is needed—to move men up front or back up men at the front—you'll find GMCs on the job 24 hours a day. From Alaska to Australia, from London to Libya, United Nations soldiers depend upon GMCs for much of their food, fuel and fighting equipment. All over America, too, commercial GMC trucks and Yellow Coaches are working night and day helping to carry peak loads of materials and workers to arsenals, shipyards and vital war production plants.

★ ★ ★ ★ ★ ★ ★ ★ ★

Truck operators can render an important service to their country by joining the U. S. Truck Conservation Corps, and by doing everything possible to prolong the life of their equipment. GMC dealers everywhere are pledged to help you carry out this truck maintenance program.

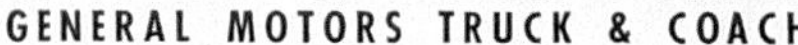

DIVISION OF YELLOW TRUCK & COACH MANUFACTURING COMPANY • *Home of GMC Trucks and Yellow Coaches • • • Manufacturer of a Wide Variety of Military Vehicles for our Armed Forces*

HERE THEY COME— enemy dive bombers screaming in for the "kill" . . . and you're a Navy gunner at the sending end of that Oerlikon 20 mm anti-aircraft cannon above! You know that a touch of your finger will hurtle 450 shells a minute into the blue . . . armor piercing shells . . . explosive shells. A stream of steel that will literally tear a plane apart in mid-air. Then you get one of the enemy airplanes in your sight . . . press the trigger . . . *and things begin to happen!* Just as they did in other naval actions where these now-famous weapons were officially commended for the number of enemy planes they helped destroy.

And whether your ship be battle wagon or merchantman, aircraft carrier or destroyer . . . the chances are pretty good that your Oerlikon is a Pontiac product. Because we've been on the job of building them since about a year before Pearl Harbor. We reached peak production months ahead of schedule. We were able to suggest changes that have made the gun more accurate in action, easier to man and maintain, more dependable when the chips are down—*and a lot less expensive for your Uncle Sam!* We realize that our part in the job of clearing the skies of enemy dive bombers doesn't begin to compare with that of the men who man the guns. *But just like them—we're giving it everything we've got!*

BUY WAR BONDS AND STAMPS

KEEP AMERICA FREE!

PONTIAC DIVISION OF GENERAL MOTORS

Every Sunday Afternoon . . GENERAL MOTORS SYMPHONY OF THE AIR—NBC Network

ONTIAC'S SIX WAR ASSIGNMENTS INCLUDE: OERLIKON 20 MM ANTI-AIRCRAFT CANNON, AIRCRAFT ORPEDOES, 40 MM FIELD GUNS, DIESEL ENGINE PARTS, TANK AXLES, TRUCK ENGINE PARTS by 1942, the Bofors intended as a replacement for the Oerlikon, though in practicality many U.S. Navy vessels employed both Oerlikons and Bofors guns. The cannon was also used by Army and Marine Corps shore-based anti-aircraft units. Approximately 30,000 Bofors 40-mm cannons were manufactured during the war in the U.S., of which Chrysler built over 25,000, the remainder by Pontiac, as shown in this ad.

Aircraft Rocket Launchers

United States Army and Navy aircraft were first armed with rocket launchers beginning in mid-1943 when the Navy used 3.5-inch rockets with a non-explosive warhead for anti-submarine work. These rockets were accurate and worked simply by having the velocity to penetrate the thin-skinned hulls of submarines. This led to the introduction in late 1943 of a 5-inch anti-aircraft shell attached to a 3.5-inch rocket, this system capable of attacking surface ships and land-based installations. However, this system was cumbersome and slowed the speed of an aircraft considerably. Thus, the High Velocity Aircraft Rocket (HVAR) was developed beginning in 1943 and produced in 1944–45. The new system was designed by Caltech scientists, consisting of a 5-inch rocket with a warhead of 7 pounds of TNT, propelled by a rocket motor. Testing was complete by D-Day and the HVAR was first utilized by P-47 Thunderbolts of the Ninth Air Force who aided the breakout from the Normandy beachhead. These rockets were powerful weapons in the hands of skilled pilots flying such fighters as the P-47, P-38 Lightning, Grumman Hellcat, and the Vought Corsair, as well as several types of Navy and Army bombers. Ordnance and weapons made of plastic during the war years were not common but, as this Celanese ad shows, they were used in making rocket launchers in order to keep overall aircraft weights down.

Aerial Bombs

A large variety of bombs were manufactured in America during the war, at least eighteen different kinds, not including experimental bombs and, of course, the atomic bomb. The casings, fuses, and other components for these bombs were built by many different companies, including the Continental Can company as shown here, and millions of bombs were dropped during the war. To discuss all these different types would require a book all their own, but their categories include general purpose bombs (the most common type), which ranged from 100-lb. bombs, dropped on enemy airfields and railroad marshalling yards, those weighing 250 lb., 500-lb. bombs designed to knock out steel bridges and concrete docks, 1,000-lb. bombs designed to knock out large steel railroad bridges and large concrete spans, the 2,000-lb. bombs for dams and large concrete and other reinforced structures like submarine pens, and the light-case 4,000-lb. bomb designed to raze an entire city block. Other categories include incendiary bombs (usually dropped in clusters), armor-piercing bombs (to sink large naval vessels), depth bombs (to sink submarines), as well as fragmentary and chemical bombs.

Torpedoes

The U.S. Navy used several different types of torpedoes during the war, fired from submarines and surface ships, as well as aerial versions launched by torpedo bombers. These torpedoes were both one of the most effective and devastating weapons of the war, but also one that encountered serious problems for the first three years of the war and led not only to many missed opportunities, but also lives being lost. The Navy's most common aerial torpedo, launched by such planes as the Devastator, Avenger, and Helldiver, was the Mark 13. Major suppliers included International Harvester and Pontiac, with some 17,000 of the torpedoes being manufactured between 1942 and 1945. The torpedo was 13 feet long and had a Torpex warhead weighing 600 lb. The Mark 13 was first available in 1936, but few were used in testing due to their high cost. However, the outset of the war quickly revealed its deficiencies in mid-1942 when results at the battles of Coral Sea and Midway by aircraft using the Mark 13 were extremely poor. The Navy's Bureau of Ordnance eventually came up with a plan to solve the many deficiencies of the torpedo, about a dozen, as well as develop a new aerial torpedo, though the later solution never came to pass. A change in tactics helped with some of the immediate problems, but it would not be until 1944 that the other deficiencies were fixed. Despite this problem, the torpedo was the main aerial torpedo used through the war and accounted for the loss of many Japanese warships. As to the torpedoes used by the Submarine Force, two were employed, the older Mark 14, and by 1943 the electric Mark 18. The Mark 14 was first used by the Navy beginning in 1931, it being nearly

PONTIAC
"IT TAKES A LOT OF HARD WORK TO WIN A WAR"

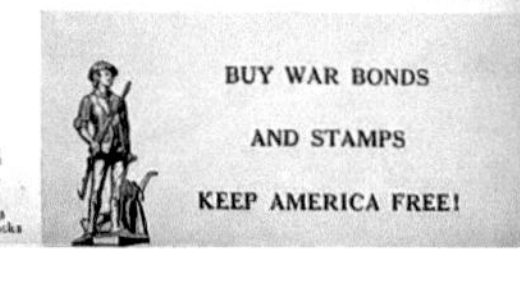
Tired muscles, taut nerves, strained hearts are part and parcel of the job of waging and winning a war. On many a front and on many a sea—wherever American youth is on the march, on the move or on the wing—they know "It Takes a Lot of Hard Work to Win a War."
And when we at Pontiac assumed the task of producing fast-firing, hard-hitting 40-mm. automatic field guns as one of our six war assignments, our craftsmen, supervisors, engineers and executives all were fully conscious of the fact that on the home front, too, "It Takes a Lot of Hard Work to Win a War."
That's why reminders, such as the one reproduced at the left above, began appearing on our plant bulletin boards. And because the need for work—unrelenting work—was inescapable, 40-mm.'s were soon rolling out to meet the Army's need. It meant "bearing down," of course. But how insignificant our efforts seem when compared to the *supreme* effort offered—and made—by our sons, husbands, fathers, brothers and sweethearts in service!
Every Sunday Afternoon . . . GENERAL MOTORS SYMPHONY OF THE AIR—NBC Network
PONTIAC DIVISION OF GENERAL MOTORS
Aircraft Torpedoes for the Navy
40-mm. Automatic Field Guns
Diesel Engine Parts
Axles for M-5 Tanks
Engine Parts for Army Trucks
BUY WAR BONDS
AND STAMPS
KEEP AMERICA FREE!

LUMARITH* E.C. in Rockets!
There's no more dramatic proof of Lumarith's toughness than its use in the advanced rocket equipment of the Thunderbolt and other famed warplanes.
Think of the great strides plastics have achieved to meet the challenges of war needs. If your peacetime production plans include the use of advanced plastics, we urge you to consult our Technical Service Department. Its staff welcomes challenging problems of reconversion.
Celanese Celluloid Corporation, a *division of Celanese Corporation of America,* 180 Madison Avenue, New York City 16.
A Celanese* Plastic

Sealing the last-minute sting in a bomb

A "block buster" bomb is harmless . . . until someone opens a "tin can."

This can contains the bomb's sting—a fuse. Without it no bomb can explode. At the last minute before a raid, the fuse is taken from the can and shoved into the nose of the bomb.

This fuse has to be *right* when it goes into the bomb. That's why it's packed in a can.

A damp fuse could turn a costly bomb into a worthless dud. But the "bomb fuse" can, moisture-proof and air-tight, keeps each fuse safe and dry until it's needed.

Vital materials like this are riding off to war by the millions in America's favorite container. They—and the can—are working for American boys, helping them do a job and come out on top. The essential things you get in cans—food, fuel, medicine—are also going to the fighting fronts in cans.

Cans are tough. They don't break, chip or tear. They protect against water, dirt, light, insects. Things get there—*safe*—in cans.

The can that goes to war today will be back again . . . guarding the things *you* depend on. It'll be better than ever, thanks to the experience we're gaining as packaging headquarters for the boys in uniform.

NOTE
TO WAR MANUFACTURERS

Metal containers are delivering the goods *safely*—foods, supplies, and bullets arrive ready for action. Continental is making millions of these cans along with other war needs, including plane parts.

Yet, rushed as we are, we can still take on more! Right now, a part of our vast metal-working facilities for forming, stamping, machining and assembly is still available. Write or phone our War Products Council, 100 East 42nd Street, New York.

CONTINENTAL CAN COMPANY

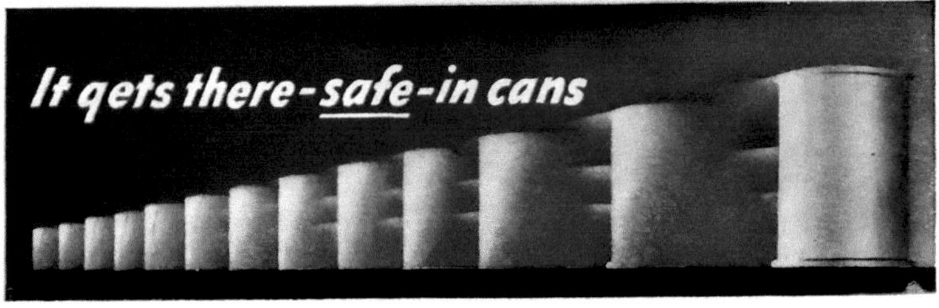

HELP CAN THE AXIS—BUY WAR BONDS

21 feet long, having a Torpex warhead which was detonated on contact or by a magnetic pistol. This underwater torpedo had a maximum range of about 9,000 yards, was powered by a steam turbine, and had a gyroscope guidance system. This torpedo was a very complex piece of weaponry, and was correspondingly expensive. Because so few were available, few were actually tested, and with war looming on the horizon, the Navy's Bureau of Ordnance had to turn to other suppliers beyond their own torpedo manufacturing sites, including the American Can Company, Pontiac, and International Harvester. Not only was this torpedo, the main weapon of our submarines, in chronic short supply, some 13,000 built during the war, but it also had several major flaws, including faulty exploders that either never worked at all, or exploded prematurely, as well as problems with the guidance system, which sometimes resulted in a torpedo making a circular run, that is traveling in a circle and coming back toward the submarine that fired it. Several U.S. submarines were lost during the war when they were struck by their own torpedo in this fashion. These torpedo problems were legion and have been well documented and written about, as any discussion about submarine performance in the first years of the war must revolve around the problems with the Mark 14. Eventually after many trials and tribulations and much Navy infighting, the problem with this torpedo was solved. While the problems with this problem were going on, the Navy also began developing the Mark 18 electric torpedo beginning in 1943. Designed and built by Westinghouse Electric, the main advantage of this type of torpedo was that it left no wake or bubbles while travelling to its target which, when observed by enemy destroyers, could be used to seek out the submarine which fired the torpedo. Initial results from this torpedo, too, were disappointing, and it had some of the same flaws, including the problem with circular runs. The top-scoring submarine of the war, USS *Tang*, is one submarine known to have been sunk as a result of such a circular run by one its Mark 18s, and it may have claimed the USS *Tullibee* as well. Like the Mark 14, these problems would be solved by 1944, and some 9,000 torpedoes of this type were manufactured during the war. Finally, there was the Mark 15 torpedo, used by Navy destroyers. It was similar to the Mark 14, but longer and had a larger warhead designed to disable or sink larger enemy warships. This torpedo, too, went through the same trials and tribulations as the Mark 14, with nearly 10,000 produced during the war. The striking ad here features a Pontiac-built aerial torpedo heading towards a Japanese carrier while the torpedo dive-bomber that dropped skims low over the water after making its glide-approach.

TIN FISH
... from the sky!

"Jap carrier and escort dead ahead."

The torpedo plane squadron wheels to deep right . . . splits into two groups to form a roaring right angle.

The Jap flat top dodges like a sluggish snake. Her guns and those of her accompanying vessels rip the bright sky to shreds.

Level and low, the Americans bore in. The carrier is bracketed. There is no escape now in all that broad sea.

"Torpedo bays open!"

"Trip 'em!"

Deliberate as death, the aircraft torpedoes seem to float down, white exhaust plumes from their turbines sharp against the blue.

They're in and under now. The mechanical wizardry of their construction rights them, drives them forward at incredible speed, straight and true, the deadliest contrivances of war known to man.

Turn! Scurry! It's no go, Tojo! Just decide on which side you want 'em.

As the planes climb sharply, their mission accomplished, the concussion of contact below shimmers against their wind screens. Tin fish . . . from the blue . . . have struck again!

The assignment to build aircraft torpedoes, one of the most complicated weapons in the history of warfare, is a tribute to craftsmanship which has been won by the Pontiac Motor Division.

For the aircraft torpedo is the "blue chip" of warfare. Weighing approximately a ton, it is capable of destroying the mightiest ship. Less than 20 feet long, from nose to rudders, it contains within its cylindrical steel walls all the powers of propulsion, navigation and destruction.

That all these self-contained qualities may be utilized, correctly and at the one precisely right moment—*without human guidance*—requires the amazing total of 5222 parts and 1225 different assemblies!

Fabrication of this amazingly complex weapon is a challenge to Pontiac craftsmanship which was eagerly accepted and which is being satisfactorily met.

The aircraft torpedo thus forms another pattern in the Pontiac-built Design for Victory on land, sea and in the air and which includes the 20 mm. anti-aircraft cannon, the 40 mm. field gun—largest automatic weapon in use by any nation—tank components, Diesel engine sub-assemblies, and vital parts for Army trucks.

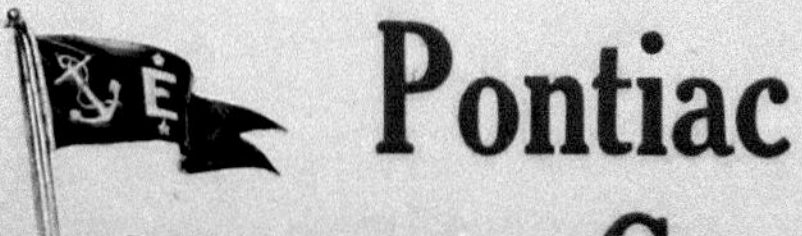

BUY WAR BONDS AND STAMPS—KEEP AMERICA FREE!

DIVISION OF **General Motors**

Source Bibliography

\303rd Bomb Group, "Aerial Bombs," www.303rdbg.com/bombs.html. March 2020.

AdAge. "1940s War, Cold War and Consumerism," March 28, 2005, adage.com/article/75-years-of-ideas/1940s-war-cold-war-consumerism/102702. December 2019.

Altherr, T. L., "Mallards and Messerschmitts: American Hunting Magazines and the Image of American Hunting During World War II," *Journal of Sport History*, Vol. 14, #2, Summer 1987.

Aron, N. R., "This daredevil fighter pilot proved that women were just as (or more) capable of conquering the skies," April 19, 2018. timeline.com/teddy-kenyon-proved-female-pilots-could-conquer-the-skies-6d0fb4467a6, February 2020.

Blair, Jr., C., *Silent Victory: The U.S. Submarine War Against Japan* (Philadelphia: J. B. Lippincott, 1975).

"Grace Line Santa Ships Resume Latin America Service," *The Log*, Vol. 41, September 1946.

Gunston, B., *The Illustrated Encyclopedia of Combat Aircraft of World War II* (New York: Bookthrift Publications, 1978); *Jane's Fighting Aircraft of World War II* (London: Random House, 2001).

Hogg, I. V., (ed.), *The American Arsenal: The World War II Official Standard Ordnance Catalog of Small Arms, Tanks, Armored Cars, Artillery, Antiaircraft Guns, Ammunition, Grenades, Mines, etcetera* (London: Greenhill Books, 2001).

Jackson, D. D., "The American Automobile Industry in World War II," usautoindustryworldwartwo.com, March 2020.

Johnson, E. R. "OS2U Kingfisher: Workhorse of the Fleet," www.historynet.com/workhorse-of-the-fleet.htm, March 2020.

Knoblock, G. A., *African American World War II Casualties and Decorations in the Navy, Coast Guard and Merchant Marine* (Jefferson, NC: McFarland & Co., Inc. Publishers, 2009).

McGowan, S., "The Boeing B-17 Flying Fortress vs. the Consolidated B-24 Liberator," warfarehistorynetwork.com/2017/06/30/the-boeing-b-17-flying-fortress-vs-the-consolidated-b-24-liberator/. April 2020.

Meek, B. A., "And the Injun goes 'How': Representations of American Indian English in white public space," *Language in Society*, vol. 35, #1, January 2006.

Ness, L., *Jane's World War II Tanks and Fighting Vehicles: The Complete Guide* (London: HarperCollins, 2002).

Neubrech, W. L., and Schumacher, A. C., "The Pulp and Paper Industry in War and Peace," *Survey of Current Business,* December 1942.

Nye, L., "These were the helicopters of World War II," April 23, 2019. www.wearethemighty.com/history/military-helicopters-of-wwii?rebelltitem=3#rebelltitem3. March 2020.

Preston, A., *Jane's Fighting Ships of World War II* (London: Random House, 2001).

Shockley, M. T., "Working for Democracy: Working-Class African-American Women, Citizenship, and Civil Rights in Detroit, 1940–1954," *Michigan Historical Review*, vol. 29, #2, Fall, 2003.

Stoff, J., "When Republic Aviation Folded," www.airspacemag.com/military-aviation/when-republic-aviation-folded-69197851/, March 2020.